Tales *from the* Heart *of* Haiti

Patti M. Marxsen

Tales from the **Heart** of **Haiti**
Author and cover artwork: Patti M. Marxsen
Cover and page layout: Nathalie Jn Baptiste
© Copyright 2010, Patti M. Marxsen and Educa Vision Inc.
Coconut Creek, FL

For information, please contact: **Educa Vision Inc.**
7550 NW 47th Avenue, Coconut Creek, FL 33073
Telephone: 954-968-7433, Fax: 954-970-0330
E-mail: educa@aol.com, Web: www.educavision.com

Library of Congress Cataloguing-in-Publication Data
ISBN 13: 978-1-58432-615-1

A **Teacher's Guide** to this story collection is available in a practical, inexpensive print-on-demand format with historical background and recommended reading, as well as discussion questions, analysis frameworks, and suggested research topics for each story. Please contact www.educavision.com or place your order through the catalog.

In memory of Gwen Grant Mellon
(1911-2000)

Author's Note

My introduction to Haiti came unexpectedly, through my association with Hôpital Albert Schweitzer (HAS), a special place in the Artibonite Valley founded by Larimer and Gwen Mellon in 1956. Since my first visit to Haiti in 1997, I have learned a great deal from historians, doctors, artists, anthropologists, and friends of that not-so-faraway place. I also acknowledge my literary mentors, contemporary writers of fiction who have written so eloquently about Haiti: Madison Smartt Bell, Marie Vieux-Chauvet, Edwidge Danticat, and Dany Laferrière to name a few.

Several of the stories in this collection have been published or recognized elsewhere: *The Dove and the Mango* was a finalist in the 1999 Writer's Digest Competition; *Lullaby* earned an Honorable Mention in the 2000 Marblehead Festival of Arts Writer's World Competition; in 2002 *The Boat on the Beach* was published in *New Century Voices*, the annual journal of the Sarasota Literary Society; and *The Artist's Wife* appeared in *The Caribbean Writer* (Vol. 18) in 2004. The collection, without the later addition of *The Wanderer*, was a finalist for the 2008 Paris Prize for Fiction.

Though often inspired by real experience, these tales and the characters in them are products of my literary imagination. Haiti is a magical land of contrast inhabited by brave and resourceful people. It is fertile ground for creative invention because anything can happen there.

Patti M. Marxsen

Table of Contents

The Dove and the Mango

The earth is dusty there, a soft dust like talcum powder that clings to bare feet until they look like clay statues. Green mangoes and coconut clusters open overhead. Riots of hibiscus and bougainvillea decorate the village houses, painted in thick coats of pink, yellow, and turquoise. The valley is lush down near the river with rice paddies and banana fields. But up in the hills, near the hospital, the roads are dry and rutted. Goats scamper everywhere, kept from the houses by barriers of cacti called candelabra. There is a fragrance of smoke and roasted meat in the air that begins shortly after dawn, after the pig has been slaughtered and the women have begun to gather in the market. All day long people will come to buy fruit and cooked vegetables and roasted meat. Bread and bananas are plentiful. Children run in all directions, leaving clouds of dust suspended in walls of heat. The smell of heat, fire, dust, and roasted pig rises to your nostrils. Overhead, there is a breeze in the green shelter of a thousand mango trees.

———————————

Dr. Sophia was talking as she arranged a spray of pink hibiscus in a blue vase, adjusting the leaves to conceal a hairline crack. "But it's really not as bad as it seems," she said, glancing over her shoulder at Rosette whose large eyes filled to the brim. Dark eyes like melted chocolate. She wiped her hands on her apron, leaving a wet stain. "You see, I never really loved him. Not really. It was nothing like that." Dr. Sophia smiled weakly and turned to face Rosette. "My life is so much more than that. The hospital. The children. Now go along and enjoy your weekend. Are you still singing in church on Sunday?" Rosette nodded and smiled a little. She was known in the village for her deep, melodic voice.

Dr. Sophia moved quickly around the room, pale hands stroking the objects she loved. The linen curtains were smoothed, the painting of distant mountains aligned with the sharp edge of the door, an isolated butterfly specimen pressed in Plexiglas. She imposed a quiet order on everything around her, even the garden where doves were cooing softly at this hour from a dovecote high in the mango trees. Long vines of bougainvillea framed the curved arches of the garden wall. Thick green leaves shot from planters like fountains. At first glance it looked carelessly natural. But in the early morning hours there was a man with a broom sweeping the stone, removing seed pods, clipping away dead leaves and withered blossoms.

"Are you sure?" Rosette's eyes were pleading.

"Yes, of course. It's not important. *C'est n'est pas grave.* It was inevitable that he would find someone sooner or later, don't you think? Someone more... energetic... less burdened. It is hard work being a doctor. A doctor is always a doctor, everywhere, all the time." She sighed and took a book from the mahogany shelf. "I must read more, Rosette. I miss my books." Their eyes met, woman to woman.

Rosette left the low, stone house with a feeling of sadness for the beautiful, white doctor. She wondered what on earth had ever brought Dr. Sophia to this place, what caused her to leave New York. And as for Dr. Bonnefoy, of course she loved him. What else does one call it? There is nothing as simple as a man and a woman together. Why do these people need to call it anything at all? It is God's will. That is all there is to say. Why do *blancs* need to pretend that something important is not important? Between a man and a woman, it is always important.

That evening, Dr. Sophia showered at five o'clock and oiled her arms and legs with mosquito repellent. She sat in the garden until seven o'clock reading about Renaissance art, trying not to think about Luc. 'How is this different?' she asked herself. He might have come by for a glass of wine or he might not. I might have gone there and cooked a chicken or a cabbage. It was not such a grand thing. A little wine, a little food, a little lovemaking. And then, the hospital; in the hallways, on rounds in the wards, immersed in the stench and the pain, the wailing of new widows, the screams of mothers whose children are ill. He was there and would still be there. But they would no longer be there together. "Ah," she sighed, looking up from Raphael, "tha's" the real loss. Now I'll be alone *in there*."

A hard ache rose in her throat. "That's the real loss," she said aloud to the trees. Because a man and a woman cannot remain friends after playing at love. And in such a small, insulated place, this would be especially hard. "So hard," she whispered, not even aware of her own voice. "Impossible."

Just then a sharp object flashed through the stone arch and hit the wall of the garden. Then another. She knew instantly what it was. Boys throwing rocks, trying to get the mangoes down. Tomorrow was market day and they needed something to sell. She stood and called out, "*Arretez-vous!* Stop it!" But another heavy rock shot into the trees, scattering a pair of doves. Their wings burst through the leaves as they lifted into the sky. Then another and a peculiar noise, a squeal and rushing sound all at once. "*S'il vous plaît! Arretez-vous!*" She hurried out of the garden, down the narrow path meandering through the cluster of flamboyant trees and back around to the village. The dark-legged boys hurried away, torn shirts flapping like wings, hands clasping the golden-green fruit. She stopped and watched as they vanished, half-smiling at their resourcefulness. *"Mes zanmis..."* Her voice trailed off in Kreyòl. "My friends... " It was hardly a crime, but the rocks were dangerous.

Then, suddenly, something twitched in the darkening light. There on the path, a broken form, mangled and dirty as a lost glove. A dove, it's silky head crushed by the blow of a sharp rock, it's trembling right wing outstretched as if frozen in flight. Dr. Sophia bent down and studied the small eye, a perfect circle, like a tack pressed into the head. It was alive but shivering through it's last moment of life. "Death everywhere," she whispered. The sharp object that had been in her throat all day pushed through and suddenly her face was streaming with tears. "Oh my dear God." She lifted the broken bird carefully and carried it back to the garden where she would bury it and light a small candle. There was, it seemed at that moment, nothing so sad on earth as a dying dove.

* * *

Rosette noticed the stone marker the next morning and asked what it was. "A dove died," said Dr. Sophia, sipping strong coffee in the garden from a bone china cup. "It fell from the tree."

"The children."

"Yes."

"Evil," Rosette said without blinking. Her dark head was balanced on an elegant neck and wrapped in a pink kerchief. "Birds are not supposed to die like that."

Dr. Sophia looked up at Rosette whose eyes were full of fear. "Yes, well, it is certainly a sad thing." Her eyes were swollen from weeping; she wondered if Rosette could tell. But of course she could tell. She knows everything.

Rosette looked away from the red eyes and placed a plate of toast in front of Dr. Sophia. "You would like more coffee now?"

"No, no thank you. And no toast. Sorry." She stood up and smoothed her skirt. It would be her first day at the hospital since Dr. Luc began sleeping with the new nurse, the one from California. Rosette knows this and keeps a solemn face out of respect. "I really must go. It's a clinic day."

The words hung in the air. "It's a clinic day," she repeated. It means hundreds of people would be lined up at the door with sick children. "I'm late as it is," she said. But as she stepped toward the door, something happened. The world tilted and Dr. Sophia fell to the ground, stumbling over the wooden chair .

Rosette tried to catch her but she was too late. The doctor was on the stone patio, rubbing her knee with long, white hands. To Rosette, these fingers looked like bones with no covering of flesh. She lifted her up and into the chair. But the world was still rocking. Dr. Sophia held her head in the palm of her hand, eyes shut, face folded in pain.

"I can't stand up." She tried again and sank into the chair. "Water... a little water. Then I'll try again--"

But the water did not help and she could not stand up or walk or do anything but hold her head in one hand and grab the edge of the table with the other. Rosette stood very still, watching.

"It's like seasickness," she said. "Everything in motion."

Rosette knew in her heart that evil had entered this house and crawled into the body of Dr. Sophia like a worm burrowing in ripe fruit. She wanted to say this but held her tongue. These *blancs* believe other things; they even believe they can control such forces with books and machines. Let them believe what they like. They are, so many of them, like ignorant children. Rosette reached down and lifted Dr. Sophia into her muscular arms and carried her down the hall. As her body was placed on the bed, Sophia fell into a deep sleep without a word.

* * *

Rosette sat in a small chair at the foot of the bed watching Dr. Sophia's breathing. At first it was even, but after a while became punctuated with a small whimper, then a long exhaling sound, then silence. Outside, the cicadas rattled in the trees and in the distance there was music, Haitian music playing on a machine. It would be a hot day with rain coming later in the afternoon. Rosette thought about the washing that must be hung and dried and removed from the line before the rain began. At 10 a.m. a young visiting physician came to the door to inquire about Dr. Sophia. "She is sick in bed," Rosette said through the screened door.

The young woman was Swiss with bulging eyes and thick legs. "Sick in bed? Well, why didn't you send a note? We have a lot of people who—" but she stopped, exasperated, as she met the solid, dark gaze of Rosette. Her English was British-accented, like other Europeans who had come before her. "Oh never mind. Just let me have a look and then we'll cope as best we can. Come along now. Step aside."

Rosette gave in, leading the young doctor down the clean-swept hall, immaculate with polished mahogany walls

and a potted palm at the end. From this corridor, the walled
garden was visible and at the end of it, Dr. Sophia's room
opened like a window, pale and large. The space was filled
with light now that the shutters had been folded back. On the
low, square bed the doctor's body lay fully clothed in a cream
linen shirt and blue skirt. Her skin was pale, in spite of the
flushed, dampness of the sleeping face. Strands of dark hair
broke the softness as they outlined the forehead. The Swiss
doctor peered at the quiet body with squinting eyes and
listened carefully to Dr. Sophia's lungs, resting her ear on the
doctor's chest, as if the dry breathing could tell a story. Then
she rested her hand across Dr. Sophia's forehead.

"It looks like malaria. But surely she was taking her
pills—" She glanced over her shoulder at Rosette who stood
with hands folded. "Do you know about any pills she might
have taken?"

"*Je ne sais rien*," Rosette whispered. "I know nothing."

"The Swiss doctor turned toward the door and
charged down the hall, calling out over her shoulder. I'll send
a nurse around later with some medication. Just keep her
quiet." She stopped and looked back. "You do understand
me don't you?"

Rosette nodded, a dark silhouette in the hallway.

"Well, good then. *Au revoir.*"

Rosette nodded again as she locked the screen door.

An hour later a Haitian nurse came to the house with
medicine and told Rosette to go about her work, that she
would sit in the doctor's room and look after her. "Dr. Luc
might come later," she added.

"No," said Rosette.

"No?"

"That would be bad. Too much has happened." The
Haitian nurse looked mysteriously at Rosette. Her mouth was

painted with lipstick and her black hair was pulled into a shiny clip. The white stockings over her dark legs made them look silver, like winter frost. Rosette could see that she understood and wanted to hear more. They were from the same world, that much was plain. "Dr. Luc made pain for Dr. Sophia. Then the children threw rocks to get mangoes and killed a dove. Dr. Sophia buried the dove last night and made a marker in the garden."

"Ahhh," said the nurse. Wide-eyed.

"It is a curse. Evil. I know this is so. I know others will die because of it. You see?"

"Yes, I see what you mean." The two women stood over the bed, held together for a moment by these mysterious events. Finally, the nurse spoke. "But this medicine will make her better. Science has power too."

Rosette's eyebrows lifted in a curious way. Maybe it was true, but she was not so sure. She felt evil in the house and shuddered, even though the room was warm. "Do not send Dr. Luc."

"He is probably too busy today anyway. And this should not be a long illness. Maybe a few days."

* * *

But Dr. Sophia did not get better in a few days. She slept fitfully in relentless heat and developed a mottled red rash along her neck. Her fever increased and subsided, then rose again, so that there was always someone sitting at her bedside with a cool cloth, a bowl of water, and medicine. The word of her illness traveled through the hospital and the village, and soon people came and sat in the yard, watching the house and wondering if Dr. Sophia would die. They talked about the good medicine she had offered their children and sisters and fathers and mothers. They brought baskets of fruit and cooked leaves in the yard over an open fire. They chattered like birds, echoing the Madame Sarahs, birds that consumed whole trees on the edge of the village with their ravenous nesting.

The best nurses came and went but Dr. Luc stayed away. Dr. Sophia's absence had created much work for him, they said. He sent his prayers. The Swiss doctor came back twice and left quickly on her sturdy feet. At night, men played softly on drums and women sat on the steps of the house singing hymns until Rosette asked them to leave. "Dr. Sophia needs rest," she whispered. As they walked away, down the path, Rosette smelled the air and wondered when it would rain. It had not rained since the first day of Dr. Sophia's sickness.

On the seventh day Rosette saw Dr. Luc standing in the path at the end of the gate early in the morning. He made no move to come closer, then left like an animal whose watch had ended. An hour later a boy came to the door. *"Je m'appelle Espérance,"* he said under his breath. He trembled, unable to look Rosette in the eye. "My name is Espérance. I killed the dove and made Dr. Sophia sick." A tear escaped his downcast eye and traced a wet line over his cheekbone.

Rosette looked down at him through the screen. Espérance Mortel, she believed, the last son of the sister of Pastor Josèph. There were many children in that family and this was the last born, a skinny boy with large eyes and a smooth, curling upper lip. "Why do you come here now?" Rosette asked, searching his eyes. "There's nothing you can do here."

"To see Dr. Sophia. To bring her limes and tell her I am sorry." He pulled six limes out of his grimy T-shirt.

Rosette reared back, wiping her hands on her apron. "Dr. Sophia is ill. Too sick to eat or drink limeade. She only takes water and maybe some bread. Anyway, go away. If you made her sick, it's too late to be sorry."

"No," he pleaded. "Please. Do not send me away. Let me see her. Let me speak to her for one minute."

Rosette took a deep breath. One minute was not too long. But what would he have to say? There was work to do in the kitchen and laundry to hang on the line. These days of extra people in the house had left her weary.

"I want to tell her that it was me and say that I will work for her now, as long as she likes."

Rosette sighed and opened the door and let him in, her eyes still and troubled. He was small but probably 16 years old, probably malnourished as a child and still not getting enough to eat. She would offer him bread before he left, but first she led him down the hall into the room where the pale blue curtains were drawn and the fan whirred slowly overhead. The room was warm and the warm air circulated like a bird flying in slow circles, stirring the curtains gently. Mosquito netting fell over the bed from one gathering point on the ceiling. And beneath it Dr. Sophia slept, dark hair pushed away from her feverish face.

"She is sleeping. She probably cannot hear you. But you may go ahead and speak. She may remember when she wakes up."

The boy winced as he gazed upon the still, closed face through the gauze of mosquito netting. He had never seen a *blanc* sick before, never seen the pale skin so bright and damp. It looked soft and spongy, like bread dough. He looked up at Rosette.

"Go ahead. Speak."

After a moment, he opened his mouth and spoke in halting English, even though Dr. Sophia spoke French and Kreyòl. It was a sign of respect, he had been taught, to try and communicate with *blancs* in their own language. "Dr. Sophia. I am Espérance. I killed a dove with rock. I throw the rock to get mango to eat. I am sorry for your sickness. I want to help you, to work for you for nothing but food. I do whatever you need. I hope I am make you well." He paused and added, "Please forgive me."

After he spoke he stepped back to stand next to Rosette and watch the still figure lying flat in the bed, covered with a light blue sheet, distant through the netting like a dark-haired fairy princess. Suddenly, the figure moved, a slight twitch of the left arm, then of the mouth. The mouth opened as if trying to speak, as if trying to form the "r" sound. The eyes fluttered. "ro…ro…"

Rosette stepped forward and leaned over her, taking her hand. "*Oui Madame. Je suis ici.* I am here. Many people are wishing you well and praying for you."

"es…espé…"

"Espérance is here. He feel very badly, Madame, for your suffering. Do you want him to work around the house? To help me out for a while?" She cast a sharp glance over her shoulder at the boy who took in a quick breath.

Dr. Sophia nodded as a faint, quivering smile passed over her face.

"Ah, well, then," said Rosette, standing up, straight-backed with surprise. "I will put him to work today, cleaning up the garden." She squeezed the doctor's hand. "You will be better soon. I can feel your strength."

Dr. Sophia nodded again, then fell back into silence.

* * *

After that day, the boy came early in the morning and swept the walk. He helped Rosette with laundry and hauled vegetables from the market in a *macoute* balanced on his small head. Rosette appreciated his help and fed him breakfast each day of bread with peanut butter, bananas, and juice from green oranges. After five days, Dr. Sophia was able to sit up in bed. The Swiss doctor came and read to her from a thick book and little by little, others came to visit. A note arrived from Dr. Luc: "Glad you are well. Luc." She smiled and put the note in a drawer.

"He is sorry now?"

"Sorry?"

"He stole your strength." Rosette's face went stiff as she placed a fresh pillow behind Dr. Sophia's neck.

Eight days after the appearance of Espérance, Dr. Sophia walked around the garden with Rosette cutting hibiscus blossoms with a kitchen knife. She sat in the heat drinking strong coffee. "Have I tasted this before? It is wonderful!" she laughed. Espérance placed large slices of melon on a wide leaf in front of her. "I honestly don't remember coffee ever tasting so good. And you, Espérance, you have saved my life. You are my protector."

The boy smiled proudly, avoiding the doctor's eyes.

Soon, Dr. Sophia went to the hospital and worked for half a day. Then a full day. Then she seemed well again and soon everyone forgot that she had been ill. Dr. Luc rushed past her in the hall. The nurses rolled their eyes at her demands like they used to, and the patients streamed into her office, dull-eyed and burdened with sick children, machete wounds, or inexplicable sores. One evening she was sitting in the garden, writing a letter when Espérance came out of the trees and stood nearby. "*Bonsoir, Madame.*"

"*Bonsoir, mon ami.* It's late for you to be here, *n'est-ce pas?*"

"You are well now, no?"

"Yes. I am well. But, you know, it was never your fault."

"Oh yes. I killed the dove to eat mango."

"I know. But I'm not sure that's why I was so sick, even though it made me sad. I think it was something else, something called *microbacteria.*"

He laughed. "You were sick with sadness, Madame."

She stared at the boy, saying nothing. His feet were bare and dirty, his arms muscular and fragrant with jasmine from clipping the bushes.

"Now that you are well, I must go away."

"Away?" She sat up straight.

"My uncle has a farm and needs help. He has goats and fields. If I work hard and earn money, he will send me to school."

Dr. Sophia stood up and walked to the edge of the garden where he stood, just over the wall, half-cloaked in feathery trees. "Please stay," she said quietly. "I need you here. You can go to school here. I can help you."

"I need to work like a man." He looked at the ground and then up into her eyes. "*Je reviens.* I will come back." He paused as if holding his breath, then disappeared into the trees, moving so fast, so suddenly that the trees shook and the branches released a fluttering of birds. Dr. Sophia stood alone in the garden, looking upward at the sound, at the rush of wings that carried everything away. She looked down the path and up again until her thoughts scattered like mist and disappeared in the evening sky.

"He is gone," Rosette spoke flatly from the shadow of the door. "*Il est parti.*"

"Doves too. Gone with him."

"*Tout change, mais on continue,*" said Rosette. "Everything chages, but we carry on." She turned back to the kitchen, wiping a bowl with a cloth.

Sophia remained in the garden, watching the sky. Soon the sky would turn dark and starry, cloaking the world in the healing silence of night. Drums would start around ten o'clock, eliciting the spirits who watch over the world and its people. Some would not survive this night, others would awaken with prayers of gratitude on their lips. Flocks of doves would return and, eventually, the boy would reappear on the path, transformed into manhood.

When he did return, and long before that, Dr. Sophia remembered those feverish days of semi-consciousness as a strange crossing, a time when her body had become a small boat navigating toward the shores of survival. She had encountered this phenomenon before in patients who gained a mysterious immunity to suffering after a long, serious illness. She had seen them walk away from the hospital, suddenly resistant to new viruses, grateful to be alive, no longer susceptible to symptoms or pain. She knew that with or without faith, those who survive are often stronger than before, but always closer to the presence of death.

Metamorphosis

There is a place along the road to the hospital where the whole valley stretches out before your eyes like a green hammock slung between one end of the sky and the other. It comes as a surprise after miles of hard driving, barren mountains, warm wind from the road; after vast fields of sugar cane and banana plants. It marks a startling shift in the atmosphere. At this point, the drivers descend slowly onto a road so full of potholes that the ride is smoother in the gutters than on the road itself. They maneuver around the potholes like dancers, daring each other from a distance. The drivers like to go fast on the Route Nationale to see who can cover the 60 miles between the hospital and Port-au-Prince in less than three hours. Then they reach this place where the road rises then dips, sinking into the valley. A child waves with both arms calling. "Blan! Blan!" even though the presence of whites is not such a strange sight here where so many come to help, year after year. Still, the child calls and people bathing in the river turn with skeptical eyes. They turn in the sun to look up for a moment, then return to the river, disinterested as if cows were passing, even if they know it is the doctor who has passed, the one they believe can bring the dead back to life. He is a good one. His long hands are always ready to lift a sick child or teach a volunteer how to stitch a wound, clean and neat, so that it heals without a trace.

The leaves, the leaves, a thick rush of leaves flew in his face like black shells, hatching in darkness. He knew the path along the canal, each rut and jutting branch. Soon the ground would open up and flatten out. The wide, overlapping leaves of almond trees would stop and lift into a feathery canopy of flamboyant trees where a carpet of bright red petals scattered beneath his feet on summer walks. Just beyond that sudden opening toward the dark sky, just across from there on the edge of the canal, he would leave her. He knew the place. God, the weight of her humid body pulled on him like a yoke. He could not distinguish between her blood and his own sweat, the slippery dank smell rising in the night air. The stench of violence and death made him stumble, even though he knew the path. He bent low like an animal to avoid the blinding leaves, her arm a dead weight dragging along the ground.

Thunder rumbled overhead. Thank God, there would soon be rain and all of this would be washed away, flushed from the earth, turned to mud, and reinvented in tomorrow's light. No footprints, no evidence other than her large, lifeless body. And the long wound at her neck. It would frighten people, that wound. He felt sorry for that. It would frighten them all around for miles along the canal, in small villages, and up into the mountains. They would talk about this for a long time, this mysterious death, Mireille's body cut open and left along the bank of the canal, floating in a thicket of reeds after a storm. He was sorry for the fear it would cause because he knew it would never happen again, not like this. He stopped to catch his breath, adjusting her weight. Her odor filled his head. He cradled her, holding her close like a child. In the dim moonlight he could see her exposed breast with its dark center.

He winced at the gaping wound. It had been necessary, damn it. No choice. He had seen it coming for over a year. At first he denied her emotions, then he only denied himself at the center of them, then resigned himself to this. He had looked at her a hundred times feeling the presence of death in the stillness of her eyes. Her dark beauty, her deep anger announced the coming of death. Unavoidable. He took a deep breath and kissed her long neck, ripped open by the blade of the knife. It was a neat cut, maybe too neat, too precise. He groaned softly. That would reveal something to an astute eye.

The clearing came soon, the cathedral-like cover of flamboyant trees arching overhead. Dark shadows. Dark sky. Just beyond, maybe thirty feet, was a deep nest of wet reeds, an oval pool almost separated from the canal by a large rock jutting into deeper water. He hurried toward it and stepped into it, into the water, into the sponge of wet grass and darting waterlife. Then he let go, settled her there in the water like an inflatable raft. Time stopped as he caught his breath, gathering it in slowly, feeling his lungs expand. Mireille sank into darkness, into shadows and soft striations of moonlight through tall, ancient trees. He watched her go, released her into a kind of weightlessness as his muscles loosened. It was then that he noticed the locusts screaming in the trees, a high-pitched chorus like a thousand whistles. A bullfrog croaked in the darkness. In the distance, he could hear a soft drumbeat. Goodnight, Mireille. It was like putting a child to bed, a sweet caress of eyes across her body and then he turned, stepping away from her, into the canal.

The water was bad but it would wash away the sweat, the blood and heat of her body. Bad water to wash away bad things. He held his mouth shut and splashed water onto his neck and his bare chest. At least it was cool. He flung his arms to chase away mosquitoes. He was half naked and pale, a light-skinned man in the canal at midnight flinging small sheets of water into the air. He swam to the bank and crawled onto the path, welcoming the first rain drops, fat and thick like spit on his back. Thank God, thank God. By the time he got back to the house the sky was crashing around him. He removed his pants, walked past the mirror, and showered in darkness. He could not look at himself yet, the face of death, the body of a murderer. Water would wash away all sins, making everything new.

Dr. Luc stood in the shower for a long time and wept a little. He would have to bury the knife but he would do it later. Not tonight. He would have to burn the pants, maybe the shoes. But he would decide tomorrow. Sunday. No maid in the house. That would give him time to clean everything up. Tonight he needed rest. Peaceful, blessed sleep beneath the pale mosquito net, the gentle humming overhead fan, a new coolness after the rain. No dreams, please God. No nightmares. No thoughts. As he closed his eyes, Dr. Luc Bonnefoy wished for silence all around. Sleep came slowly with the sound of rain on leaves.

* * *

He was thinking of that night, reliving the humid sensation of death because the sky was rumbling in thunder and Mireille's daughter was standing at the gate. He had not seen the girl in a long time and barely recognized her at first. She was no longer a girl, but a young woman now with her mother's deep eyes and ballerina posture. Her head was balanced on a glossy, graceful neck like a prize melon, her body full and elegant with long arms and solid legs. So much like her, he thought as he walked toward the wooden gate, leaving a woman on his couch watching from the window, composing his features as he approached the girl. When he lifted the wire and pushed the slats back, her eyes shifted downward out of respect and shyness.

"Bonsoir, Yvette."

"Bonsoir, Dr. Luc." She smiled slightly, still refusing to meet his eyes. "They say you need a cook." She spoke Kréyol with a crisp, delicate voice.

"Yes. Lunise has left to go to Port-au-Prince."

"I am a good cook." She met his eyes with this statement.

He imagined what it would be like to have Yvette in the kitchen every day, to watch her moving to and from the table, clearing breakfast dishes, bringing coffee out to the garden, balancing *macoutes* of fruit and vegetables on her head to bring into his house. Mireille's daughter. The same high behind and perfect head. "Have you worked as a cook before?"

"Yes. With Madame Morency, before she returned to Canada."

"Ah." Madame Morency was the wife of a visiting doctor, known for her good taste. He had dined at her table, not knowing who had prepared the food, but remembering a piece of fish glistening with rich, spicy sauce.

"Do you know how to bake bread?"

"Yes. Good bread from the oven."

"When are you available?"

"Tomorrow." She spoke softly.

"No, I don't need anyone here on Sundays. But come Monday and plan to work five days a week plus Saturday morning. We'll see how it works out. And you must get along with Solange, my maid."

"Okay." Her mouth widened into a smile. "I will do good work."

"I'm sure you will, Yvette." He moved to close the gate then opened it again. "Yvette."

"Oui."

"How old are you now?"

"I am sixteen." Her eyes flickered, nearly meeting his curious gaze.

"I remember your mother."

"Yes. It is eight years now. But I remember her too."

"Yes. Eight years."

* * *

Evelyn was watching from the window as he came back to the house. Thank God it's going to rain, she thought, as she studied his enigmatic expression. He was a quiet man, largely buried inside himself, but they had found a small place together. These evenings of wine and talk, Bach, and occasional lovemaking had become more and more frequent. She felt a wave of desire as he looked up, meeting her eyes overlayed with the reflection of the dark girl receding down the path. He smiled and mouthed "Evelyn" and she laughed deeply, from the throat.

"Who was it?" She stood, handing him a fresh glass of wine, golden Chardonnay from an air-conditioned supermarket in Port-au-Prince. The coolness of the wine formed a mist on the glass.

"A girl named Yvette. My new cook. I knew her mother. She was my maid for a while. She died several years ago." He arranged his face and sipped the wine. *"C'est bon."*

"At the hospital?"

"No. She was murdered." He looked up and saw in Evelyn's blank face a curiosity for more information. There is nothing as lovely as an intelligent, curious woman, he thought. "Her throat was cut and her body left in the canal. Some mysterious piece of village justice, I imagine."

"Murder? Really?"

"How long have you been here now?"

"Three years."

"Yes, well, these local feuds, they go on for years... sometimes generation to generation. Revenge. Justice. Call it what you will."

"But why would anyone kill a young mother? A maid?"

"Who knows. Yvette is not the only child and usually there is more than one father."

"Of course." Evelyn poured more wine and dismissed the mystery of Yvette's mother. "It's odd, because I feel so safe here myself. Immune, almost, from violence."

"Oh, you are. At least I believe you are... these things... they're always amongst the people. They have nothing to do with us, really." He smiled and replaced a fallen piece of her hair, tucking it into the soft elastic at the nape of her neck. She blushed a little, feeling like a girl. "Let's talk of happier things," he said, still smiling. "Let's listen to music. What would you like? Vivaldi? Chopin? Bach?"

"Vivaldi, of course!"

* * *

Yvette came to the kitchen door at 6 a.m. on Monday morning and began by squeezing juice from thick, green oranges. Then she made strong coffee and fried eggs and covered the eggs with corn flakes from a large box. Solange explained that she would tend the house and that there was no need for Yvette to enter all the rooms, especially Dr. Luc's study or his bedroom. She held her crooked finger out in Yvette's face and said that no matter what happened, no one was to touch the butterfly collection or take the fine, leather-bound books from the shelf, that only Dr. Luc could touch those things. Yvette nodded, open-mouthed. All she wanted was enough money to buy shoes for her brothers and sisters and give some money to her aunt so that she would not be thrown out of the house. She did not say it, but she did not care about Dr. Luc's butterfly collection or the books.

* * *

A week later Dr. Luc came home late on Friday night. His back hurt from bending over the operating table during a long surgical procedure and he was hungry. As he approached the house, he wished for a moment that Evelyn might be there to lift his mood. Her body was in his mind as he walked through the gate. The Brandenburg Concertos were playing. That was odd. Perhaps Evelyn was there. But soon, he realized that only Yvette was at home, waiting patiently in the kitchen with warm bread and eggplant casserole and stewed chicken and beans.

"The music?" he asked sharply.

"I was lonely and it was all I could think of." Her eyes were filled with dread. "I know how to work the machine from watching you," she added, hoping to reassure him.

He scratched his head absently. "Oh, well, it's all right. In fact it's nice to come into a house filled with music… and food. But you didn't have to wait, you know." He stared at her for a long moment. Her eyes were dark and liquid like her mother's, her proud shoulders held inward as if to shield herself. "Really, Yvette. There was no need."

"I'll put your dinner on the table if you like."

"Yes, fine. Just give me a few minutes to wash."

The dinner was good. Yvette served him silently then went back to the kitchen. She came back to clear the dishes and asked if he wanted coffee. He preferred rum tonight so she brought that in a small glass with two ice cubes and set it near the couch on a low, mahogany table. He stretched out there and closed his eyes while she worked in the kitchen, wrapping leftovers and wiping the counter. Then she came back to the salon and asked if he wanted more rum. He watched her as she bent to pick up the glass and, almost instinctively, touched her arm.

She stopped and looked at his face, avoiding the eyes. "Do you want me to kiss you?"

"Yes. Oddly enough, I do."

"Did you ever kiss my mother?"

Suddenly he sat up and wiped his face with his hands. "My God I'm so tired! Get out of here, Yvette! Get out! You're done for the day and I'm just too damn tired! Get out! Go! Go now!"

The girl hurried into the kitchen with the empty glass and left through the back door. Dr. Luc Bonnefoy sat in his salon, staring at the floor, listening to the charging strings of Bach.

* * *

The girl returned the next morning to prepare breakfast, but Dr. Luc did not want anything other than coffee. He took a large mug of it into the study where his butterfly collection was arranged in covered glass trays of thick cotton. It was not a large collection, less than 50 specimens, but the vibrant wings electrified the room. Orange and yellow. Swallowtails and tiger stripes. A whole tray of chartreuse and black, the most common coloration in the valley. He looked them over with satisfaction, thinking he might go for a walk the next day, into the mountains, and try to find something new, untouched, unusual.

"Did you wish more coffee?" Yvette stood at the door with the glass pot. Looking up, he could see that her sweet face needed something from him. He smiled and went to her, holding out his mug.

"You have been a good girl, Yvette. And I know you have never come into this study, have you?"

"No, Dr. Luc. Solange said I must not do that." Her breath was sweet and her voice excited.

"Do you like butterflies?"

"I would like to be a butterfly." She spoke with a solemn expression but he laughed and led her into the room.

"Let me read something to you." She stood still with folded hands as he read from a large, flat book. "*The transformation from a larva to a pupa is one of the more dramatic events in nature, familiar even to many people who know little else about butterflies. Within a few minutes the old larval skin is split, and the new pupal skin emerges from underneath. This pupal skin rapidly hardens, and provides a protective barrier around the soft parts as they undergo a dramatic transformation and reorganization inside, changing from the old organization as an herivorous, walking caterpillar to the organs of the nectar-feeding, flying, adult butterfly. When the metamorphosis inside the butterfly pupa is complete, one day the pupal shell splits, and the adult butterfly crawls out.*"

He looked up triumphantly. He was breathing rapidly and a rim of sweat appeared on his forehead.

"Look," he said, taking her hand and guiding her to one of his butterfly cases. "Look at these magnificent colors. Would you like to wear these colors?"

"Oh yes. I would!" They both laughed.

When he turned to her and took the pot from her hand she froze, still as a statue. Then he kissed her and she trembled. Her eyelids were fluttering like wings, their thin membranes covering her soul.

"I want to make love to you too. You know that, don't you?"

"Yes."

"Can you keep a secret if we do? Can you promise to tell no one?"

"Yes."

"Solange is off today. Will you come with me now?"

"Yes."

* * *

Six months later when Yvette left the valley, people wondered how she had made enough money in the village to go to Port-au-Prince all by herself. A relative, some said. A *blanc* who knew her mother. Dr. Luc's generosity, said others. There were rumors of a child coming but no one claimed the child. No one claimed Yvette. Many people said this is what happens without a mother to teach a girl. Hey, maybe she'll make it big and come back here, someone cackled, and they all laughed because that never happened.

She stood alone waiting for the bus in a straight orange dress with a black sash. Her breasts had grown larger and hung heavy in the bodice, pulling her neck out of line. Then Solange came along with a bag of banana chips and a Coca-Cola to share. Two days before, Dr. Luc had given Yvette an envelope that she had tied into her bodice, close to her body. She promised never to return in exchange for this envelope and smiled as he kissed her hand. No one had ever done that before. She kissed her hand later in the same spot before she washed in the river. He said he thought they understood each other. She nodded, staring at him with dark eyes until he had to look away.

"I won't forget you," he said, "you are my butterfly."

When the bus came, Yvette looked suddenly at Solange before she pulled herself up into the narrow space. There were so many people, all loaded down with plastic sacks and baskets full of food and clothes and live chickens. Yvette squeezed into a seat and looked out at Solange who was nodding and trying to smile as her eyes turned bright and wet. Yvette's hand rested on her belly, knowing that she would love whatever was inside of her. "Don't cry," she whispered, as if Solange could hear her, or maybe she was talking to the baby.

It was too bad that love had to be taken the way she took it from Dr. Luc. It was almost like stealing because she knew he would never have given her this gift if she had asked for it, this life unfolding now in the cocoon of her body. And once it was done, she knew she had to go away. Yvette pressed her hand to the window and Solange nodded bravely. Maybe she would name the baby Solange, if it turned out to be a girl. Or maybe she would name the child after her mother. "Bye bye Solange!" They waved at each other with silent palms spread wide.

When the bus left the village, turning toward the dusty road, Dr. Luc was high in the mountains hunting new specimens to add to his collection. When he returned, he would not mind the quiet in the house. And when it began to bother him again he could always listen to music. It was there waiting at his fingertips; the soothing touch of Chopin, the wild, discipline rhythms of Bach on a hot night.

The Boat on the Beach

The western shore of the island is dotted with beach clubs hidden behind walls and wrought iron gates that open onto the Route Nationale. They say "Baby Doc" Duvalier used to come up here to the beaches, to his private house, throwing lavish cocaine parties on weekends. From his rooms and his balcony he would have seen this same turquoise sea, the same waves shimmering in the heat of the day then cooling with the sun's sinking. The sand must have been hot beneath his feet as he walked to the water's edge, just as it is today. Too hot to walk on, rocky and coarse. He might have scanned the horizon with his cruel eyes and seen the same sky, the same island out there. And before him, years and decades and centuries before him, there were others who came to these beaches and swam naked in these waters to feel clean, to wash away the day's dirt, sweat, blood, and suffering. Like us, they must have eaten meat and fruit after a redeeming swim. They, too, must have felt the sting of sunburnt skin and feared the deep humidity of night.

She walks away from the hotel in the morning sun, sarong fluttering like the loose wing of a dying insect, away from the straw mat of banana leaves, away from the book splayed open, face-down. She is one of only six guests this morning. Others will come along this afternoon. They come every weekend from Port-au-Prince, checking into air-conditioned rooms, leaning over balconies of ocean front hotels to escape the terror of the city, to rest. *Au Dela* is a small resort with 25 rooms connected to a thatched pavilion where drinks and meals are served and a small Caribbean band plays nonstop until midnight. It is not one of the fancy places but, like the others, it is a separate place from the rest of the country, from the other side of the gate.

She walks slowly up the beach, watching the sea through dark glasses, following the arc of the water's edge past the beach club property onto a private beach, toward a small dock. Beyond the dock there is a promontory, gray-green in the distance and fringed with tall palms bending toward the sea. Beyond that, out of view, there is a town of pink and white and pale blue buildings. She knows the town, but enjoys the fact that it cannot be seen from here. It is a busy coastal town, anchored in the center by a shady, fenced-in park. The square is crowded with shops and street vendors, dance clubs, churches, and lottery shops. There are even a few restaurants where you can sit in the shade and have large platters of fish and rice brought out with cold beer or Coca-Cola. She knows this place because she has spent the past three weeks living there in a guest house behind a mansion owned by the American brother of one of the town's most successful merchants. The American brother has arranged to sponsor an exhibit and pay her $5,000 for her photographs of children. She is a photo-journalist with the assignment of spending one month among the children of Haiti and returning with photographs, hundreds of them.

She thinks about these children as she walks alone, away from the hotel. She is not young, but moves in an elegant line, swaying slightly in the stiff breeze. She sees their faces everywhere now, the undernourished, the dusty ones, the small ones hauling water uphill with no shoes, the dull-eyed babies sucking their mother's flat breasts. Last week she went to an orphanage in Port-au-Prince. The pictures of that place are the worst, she thinks, the best pictures of the worst conditions. Even worse than the hospitals, which are places of hope. She thinks about the faces of the children as she walks along the beach, wondering how she will limit the exhibition to 50 or 100 pictures. She has already taken over 1,000 photographs.

Just past the dock, she stops and turns, full face to the sea vibrating in the heat. She might burn today, though her skin has adapted somewhat and she is covered in expensive sun lotion, SPF 30. Her shoulders glisten and her sarong billows as she faces the sea with 1,000 images of children in her head. Maybe the exhibit will be limited to Laughing Children. Or, perhaps, Dying Children, though she imagines Dr. Gérard would not like that approach. After all, it is his money. He should have something to say about it. Maybe she can get some grant money and publish a book to go along with the exhibit. Then she could show more, lay out chapters on Laughing Children, Dying Children, Children at Work, Children Learning, and so on. Her head is filled with ideas and images that filter through the blinding heat. Her eyes water from the intensity of light on water.

This was to be a time of rest, a time away from the camera and the dark room and the noise of St. Marc, the town on the other side of the promontory. Lunise, Dr. Gérard's sister, has been very kind but was expecting company this weekend. It seemed a good time to leave for a while. It was tiring for everyone having a single American woman around, especially one with a camera slung around her neck. "They will fear your camera," Dr. Gérard had warned. "They believe it gives you power over them to have their image. So be sure to ask and respect those who refuse to be photographed." He shook his dark finger in her face with that warning. "Don't forget."

She walked back up the beach in the opposite direction. There was a cluster of almond trees at the edge of the hotel property and someone had placed a bench there in the shade of the trees. As she sat down and watched the horizon, the breeze flared up, showering her with scarlet petals from the flamboyant trees growing close to the two-story building. She smiled and twirled a soft petal between her fingers. What unexpected beauty. She closed her eyes, imagining herself in a small car, driving fast, rushing toward something she could not see. Things seemed that way before she left the city. It was all just out of reach, but everything felt so close. She blinked, looking up, and noticed a dark spot on the water, faraway but moving closer toward some slow, inevitable collision with the shore. It was a small boat, a *pirogue*, a hollowed out log with what appeared to be one man rowing. She watched and waited. He must have come from Gonâve, that mysterious hump of an island across the bay where the poorest of the poor are said to live. It was a long way to come alone in a small boat.

As he approached land, she could see that he was the only man in the boat, but there was something else moving, a strange silhouette with a polished golden streak flashing in the sun. A dog? A goat? She watched and waited until she could see the colors and the plumes, magnificent like a turn-of-the-century hat. It was a rooster with a rope around his neck, secured to the bow and sitting upright and curious at the end of this long journey. The boat surged forward with swollen waves. When the rocky bottom was visible through the clear water, the dark man removed his shirt and dove into the water, submerging his head for a moment then bobbing up and shaking it like a dog after a bath. He said something to the rooster, then pulled the boat ashore, up onto the rocky sand, directly in front of the woman standing on the beach in a dark swimsuit and colorful sarong.

"Bonjour, Madame!" He smiled broadly as if his face might break with the effort, showing a square set of crooked teeth. The nose was flat and wide, the eyes dark and glittering with an idiot's joy.

She stood still as he tugged at the boat which seemed to present the rooster like a young prince. "I like your bird!"

"Heh! Heh!" The man was skinny but he laughed big. "He is good bird! He is magic!"

"Magic?"

"*Mais, oui*! I no lie to you lady!"

She stepped out from beneath the shade to inspect the rooster. It sat still except for the clenching of claws on the edge of the boat. The bird was enormous and dressed in colors so rich she thought of the embroidered vestments worn by a priest at home in her father's church. The eyes were empty and solid; the comb fleshy and red. "He is superb," she said cautiously.

"He give you three answers," the man said. He was standing under the tree now, patting his muscular chest. "Three answers. No more. You ask three questions. Okay?"

She smiled. "Three answers?"

"Oui Madame! Bird is magic. He is spirit. He know everything. You ask three questions. You get three answers. *Je vous promis.* I am lucky man to have magic bird."

She stood silently for a moment, looking from the man to the rooster, then out to sea into the hazy nothingness and the gray island in the distance. "You have come from Gonâve?"

"Oui! Gonâve! You know it?"

"No. No, I… I live in America."

"Ah! *C'est bon, ça*! That's good! You have three questions, yes?"

She hesitated, smiling weakly. It was absurd to ask a rooster for an answer to anything, totally absurd. "Well, no, not now anyway." She looked toward the hotel. There was no one else in sight. The building was mute and pasty, baking in the sun. She realized that her head hurt a little, probably from the heat. "I have some things to do. Will you be here later?"

"Oui!" His smile bloomed.

"Well, maybe I'll come back out later. Let me think about my questions and I'll come back later."

"*Pas de problème Madame!*"

She could feel the four eyes watching her as she picked up her book, walked away, and hurried up the white-washed stairs to her room. It was cool and dark inside with a hard glossy floor. She locked the door quickly, feeling something sharp and unexpected rising inside of her throat. Oh, the heat, she thought. And that poor, crazed man with his rooster. And the children. All those children. All those lives going nowhere. Her hands came quickly to her face, covering everything so her eyes and the images inside her head went blank. Suddenly, she collapsed in tears on the cool bed, clutching a foam rubber pillow as if it could bring hear her thoughts. Oh dear God, she thought, what is happening? Magic roosters and abandoned beaches and dying children. She untied the knot of the sarong and wrapped it around her shoulders, then wept herself to sleep.

It was three hours later when she woke up, nearly one o'clock, with clouds of half-remembered dreams thick in her head. With eyes still shut, she remembered herself running down a corridor chasing something, rushing toward the pinhole end of the corridor, fingers brushing long, polished walls, shiny as copper. Hurry, hurry, the voices were calling.

Yes, there was a chorus of voices urging her on, urgent voices in low unison. She pressed her shut eyes to the pillow and remembered that sound, like wind in a storm. Hurry, hurry. There was a lost child somewhere, maybe at the end of the corridor, through the pinhole. She ran faster and felt the corridor closing in, narrowing and becoming tunnel-like with a low, curved ceiling. The light dimmed; the tiny opening at the end was so far away. She was frightened, wishing for help, wishing for Alan or Mary or Dad. But they were all gone now, gone forever. The voices repeated the words in her head. Hurry, hurry!

She was running faster, stumbling into the ever-narrowing tunnel with voices ringing all around when she woke suddenly into silence except for the groaning of the air conditioner. She sat up slowly, remembering the rooster and the boat on the beach. She went to the window and could see the man and the bird, waiting patiently beneath the almond trees. Her heart dropped at the sight of them. Damn it. Of course there were questions to be asked. Why did Alan leave? What really happened to Mary that day? How much longer would she be able to do this? Where would she go next? What was she running from?

Her life was filled with questions, but who could bear to know the answers? Asking a question with a guaranteed honest answer wasn't like praying for something or even like making a wish with a penny. She shuddered and turned the air conditioner off. It was impossible to understand the past and better not to know what was coming next. In fact, it was best if no one could know, ever, not even a magic rooster. She realized as she washed her face and peered into the mirror that it was the mystery of each day that kept her going. The quest without even knowing what the quest was about. To know everything now would be death itself.

She pulled a pair of shorts over her swimsuit and grabbed her wallet and camera, arranging the leather strap around her neck, pulling her hair into a black clip. The man stood up as he saw her appear on the steps, walking toward him in a straight line. He eyed the camera suspiciously, but smiled anyway, a nervous smile. He nodded as she came closer, head bobbing up and down like a *papier mâché* puppet.

"*Bonjour, Madame!* You come back! Is good!"

"I am rested now," she said, "and I have thought about this magic *coq.*" The rooster crowed vigorously for the first time, then pecked and scratched the sand for something to nibble on.

"*Oui*? You have questions now?"

"No. No, I have another idea." She sat on the bench and folded her hands in her lap, looking up at the man. "I want you to kill him."

"*Quoi*?! What?! Kill magic bird?" The man placed both hands on his head in alarm. "*C'est impossible!*"

"Yes. I want you kill him and I will pay you to do it. Two hundred American dollars. Look. See. Here is the money I will give you if you kill him now." She opened her wallet and pulled out a small roll of bills.

His face went dark. She could see that he did not want to kill the rooster, that he believed in its magical powers, or wanted to, but she would not release him from the temptation. She held out the money in a little fan, twenty dollar bills, ten of them. American money which amounted to nearly six month's earnings or more. You could almost buy a pig for that, or at least a bicycle. You could serve the spirits with that kind of money and feed your family too. All for a dead rooster. "Here," she said. "American money. This is all yours if you kill it. In fact, kill him right here, right now, and I'll take a picture of him dead." Her mouth tightened with excitement as she spoke. Maybe there was something to this idea of capturing a spirit with photographs.

He looked nervously from the money to the rooster and back to her eyes. It would be a betrayal. That was clear enough. The fat, plumed bird twittered and jerked its head from side to side, crowing again though less boastfully. The money fluttered a little in the breeze so she had to clamp her thumb over the stack of bills. The man's eyes ticked between the money, the rooster, the money. He looked up, pleading.

"Kill bird now?"

"*Oui*. Yes, absolutely. Now." She slid the money into her pocket and stepped back as he suddenly grabbed the glistening feathered neck of the rooster. The bird squawked and struggled, but not for long. She watched it all through the window of the camera like a tiny film. She zoomed in close, then pulled back, waiting for the moment, wanting to capture the mass of colored feathers in the sunlight just at the moment of death. But that wasn't all of it. There was another picture she was waiting for, the real photograph that she would keep for a long time to remember this day, this place.

It came to her as she watched the event in miniature. She realized that she was holding this man in her hands and waiting for the look in his eyes, that flash chance Cartier-Bresson called "the decisive moment." He was a strong man with a strong grip. The rooster's neck wobbled and snapped quickly before the man looked down and tossed it toward the water. The plumes were still glorious but twitching on the beach. He watched carefully to make sure it was done. As the bird's jerking motion subsided, he touched the mass with his naked foot, scooting it into the ragged remnant of a wave.

When he looked up she saw the moment in his eyes and snapped the shutter quickly, three times. Her hands gripped the camera. Her heart was beating wildly as his face moved toward her, wincing, filling the frame with wide eyes, black nostrils. His mouth froze, unable to speak, half twisted like an old sack too stiff too close. The rooster was dead and now he wanted the money. He needed the money and he wanted it now. That was the picture—a man without choices. That was it and she got it, captured it forever, the answer and the question in one split second.

Lullaby

People gather along the roads in patches of dust and dry grass, on broken pavements, waiting for a tap-tap. They crowd into these small trucks or large busses, clinging to railings and swinging off the back. It is hard but easier than walking up and down the hills of Port-au-Prince. It is a long day in the city, with work and traffic, dust and heat, the clamor of cars and busses and beggars. People live everywhere, crowded into houses and apartments stacked like cardboard boxes in the sun. Many families sleep in shifts, sharing the beds they have among themselves.

Around the President's Palace, the houses are nicer and the streets broader. Some houses have porches, balconies, and small shaded yards. Further up, in Pétionville, there are villas with gates and views, courtyards and gardens shuttered against the teeming life of the city. It is cooler up there, especially in the morning when people sit on their balconies looking out across the city, toward the sea. Those people are like birds soaring over a vast plain. From there, no one can imagine the things that happen beneath such flight.

Georgette was in the habit of singing a lullaby to her three daughters every night. They had been born one after another, three years in a row, each fathered by a different man. This was not so unusual, but Auntie Clarisse frowned on it. Auntie was a lean, leathery woman with one son, Félix, and no one even knew who Félix's father was. So Auntie had no room to be self-righteous, even if she was a successful dressmaker with customers among the elite who lived in the hills above

Port-au-Prince. She made fine dresses for light-skinned women who swayed when they walked. "You are too beautiful when you are pregnant," Auntie said to Georgette, her brows folded in disapproval. "They see you like that and they want to be the one who made you so beautiful."

The third child, Annette, who was only two, was fathered by Hugo who drove a van back and forth to the city for a hospital in the north. He was a good man who said he loved Georgette and said he loved the child too. Hugo slept in a cinder block dormitory at the hospital during the week, but if he had to drive a doctor to the airport and wait a while to pick up the next one, he would come to the rue Capois to see Georgette and the child. It was clear from the way he smiled and hugged the little girl that he loved her very much. It even seemed to Georgette that he loved the others, not in the same way perhaps, but almost as much. They all had large brown eyes and hair twirled into dark knobs with plastic barrettes. Whenever they saw Hugo at the gate, Jacqueline, Sophie, and Annette would squeal and run to him, hugging his long legs. He would laugh and squat down to kiss each one, though it was always Annette who would be in his arms when he stood and came up the steps of the house.

"Are you alone?" he would ask, still holding the child who touched his dark, sculpted jaw with her finger.

"Papa!" she squealed, poking his face.

"Yes, Auntie has gone to a fitting in Pétionville. And Félix has been gone for days. Probably up to no good." They laughed and kissed each other in the hallway. If there was time, and the girls were playing, he would hold her against the wall, touching her slowly or lifting her skirt around him. She loved to feel him that way, his weight pressing against her in the shadows, his breath quickening on her neck.

"*Je t'aime,*" he always said, before he left. And before he got into the van, "Oh, I almost forgot. I had some extra money this week. And here is a bottle of pain pills from the pharmacy and a melon for their breakfast." Or a pineapple, or a bag of tomatoes. Hugo was a good man. He only took what he needed and always left something behind.

Georgette worked at night, when Auntie was sure to be home. She used to wait tables at the café at the airport. That's where she met Hugo. But it was hard to get there and back through all the traffic. Sometimes the only way home was in a taxi with a mean-faced driver who took the long way around and charged too much. A few times she let the taxi drivers touch her, just to get home cheap. So when she heard about the job at the hotel at the top of the rue Capois she went and sat in the garden all day waiting for the owner.

He was smooth and pale, married to a beautiful woman who sang at the hotel in a band on Saturday nights. They had two skinny boys who spent most of their summer days in the pool. When he saw her in the garden and sent for her, they talked beneath a breadfruit tree by the pool while the boys raced from one end to the other, kicking water into the air. He even had a waiter in a white jacket bring a pitcher of limeade out with tall glasses and plenty of ice. He liked her and said she could work the dinner shift five nights a week, Tuesday through Saturday. Georgette was so happy she ran all the way home, down the steep hill, and hugged Auntie with both arms right at the sewing machine, which made the old woman shriek and throw her hands into the air like palm leaves. "*Sois soigneuse!* Be careful!"

Georgette liked working at the hotel. She kept silent as she served the food, but enjoyed hearing different languages and learned a lot from the conversations she overheard. People there talked about politics and how Haiti was receiving money from all over the world, about vaccines and medicines that could bring sick people back to life, about science and history and music and God and what life was like in other countries. Serving food to such people was like having new teachers every night. She listened carefully and told Hugo everything.

"Do you know what it means, a solar eclipse?" she asked one afternoon, as they sat in the yard watching the children play with a toy that was meant to catch the wind and spin like a flower in the air. There was no wind, so the children ran around in a little circle, shaking the toy in the air.

"No. I have no idea," he said, drowsily. He had gotten out of bed at 4 a.m. in order to drive an important visitor to a 9 a.m. appointment at the European Union and was free now until 4 o'clock. This meant he would not get back to the hospital until after dark. He worried about driving that road after dark, but never complained to anyone.

"It means something about the sun and the moon taking away light," she said. "I think it must be evil."

"Hmm?"

"*Oui.* The moon gets in the path of the sun and the light vanishes. It is very dangerous, I think. I heard them talking about it last night."

Hugo touched her back. He loved her silky skin and was pleased that she found her job so interesting. "Dangerous?"

"I think so. Don't the doctors know about it at the hospital?"

"I don't listen to them much, if they do."

"You should listen. Or maybe you should ask. I am worried about this thing, this solar eclipse." Her voice faded away softly, so Hugo opened his eyes and looked at her. He could see the fear there and stroked her back again. "I want to know more about it," she added, rising to pull a leaf from Annette's mouth.

"Why? What are you afraid of?"

She stood with her back to him, so his hand hung empty in the air. "I don't like this thing. It steals the light. Don't you understand anything!" She turned and their eyes met. He was good and handsome, but something about him was too calm. Nothing bothered him. She covered his eyes with a big almond leaf. He snatched it away and threw it on the ground.

"Stop it! And don't worry," he said. "Antoine gave me some new pills to help you sleep. Here, put these in your purse." He pulled a tiny plastic sac from his pocket with ten white capsules in it. She sighed and took them, pushing the sac deep into the pocket of her skirt.

Later that evening, two doctors from Switzerland climbed into the van and shook hands with Hugo. At first they said little, then they began to talk about how dry it was, how brown the mountains were, and how crowded the road going out of Port-au-Prince had become since their first visit five years ago. Then one of them said the word "eclipse" and the other nodded, agreeing that Haiti was right in line to experience the strange darkness of a "total solar eclipse."

"It will be like midnight at noon," one of them said. The other spoke of stinging flashes of light, of beads of light. Hugo imagined Georgette in a necklace made of glowing beads. Then he asked a question. "This is bad, this eclipse?"

No, no, no, they said. There's nothing bad about it, just unusual. "Happens every twenty years or so."

"That often?"

"I believe so, somewhere, but not likely here."

Hugo listened and nodded. He did not understand why it was so important, why it was happening in Haiti, or when this strange darkness at noon would occur. He stared straight ahead at the road, thinking of Georgette's troubled eyes and dark face, plump as a melon, of glowing beads around her neck, of her hips beneath her skirt.

A few days later there was talk of the total solar eclipse on the radio. Then he saw a newspaper splayed open on the sidewalk at the airport with an article on the eclipse. There was a picture next to the article, a black disc surrounded by a ring of fire. People were worried. "But it's not bad," he told the girls in the restaurant near baggage claim. "It's just something in the sky."

They shook their heads at this. Mireille, the tall one who gave him extra butter with his toast, said her old grandmother had lived through one before and it was evil. "It's the devil's cloak, according to her. And if you are standing around outside in the middle of it, you go blind. You wait and see." Her face was solemn.

Even Auntie Clarisse was hearing talk of the total solar eclipse in the cool hallways of her customers' homes. She told Georgette it would be next Tuesday, all day long, and to stay inside and keep the children quiet. "I'll hang dark fabric on the windows so we won't get shot through with stinging light," she said. "I'll stay in my bed all day and stay quiet. Is best not to move around too much, don't let this evil thing know you are here."

Georgette listened and made her plans. If Auntie was going to stay in her bed all day in a dark room, she would make a soft place on the floor in the front room and keep her daughters there. She would stuff fabric and tissue paper in the windows and around the cracks of light in the doors and wear her sunglasses under a straw hat. She would dress herself and the children in long-sleeved clothing. But how would she keep them still? How would she keep them from running out onto the porch to play?

"You pray to keep them still," Auntie said, her voice gaining force with each word. "You pray for God's grace on that day. You pray your body don't explode with stinging light on that day. They say it will be total darkness at noon except for stinging light, and it will come slowly like a man come from the shadows to grab you." Her breath was sour and hot as she spoke.

Georgette wished Hugo would come and hold her in the hallway, touching her legs and telling her he loved her. Auntie Clarisse's face was full of fear. Georgette looked away, toward the window, and saw her daughters running around the tree outside in a circle, laughing and kicking up dust. "I wish…" but she did not finish her thought. Auntie stood very still, except for her eyes that traveled the room in a suspicious orbit. "Don't wish, you stupid girl, you *pray*."

The night before the solar eclipse Georgette kissed her daughters and made them lie down on the stack of pillows and cotton coverlets in the salon. She said she would sing them a special lullaby if they would taste something for her. They sat like birds in a nest with their mouths open, necks craning up toward Maman. Georgette pressed the pills Hugo had brought between two spoons to make a powder, then she stirred the powder into mashed banana and sat down with her little girls, spooning the mixture into their mouths from a bowl. "More, more, you must have more," she said. They were hungry and they liked the mashed banana so she made another bowl of it and they ate it eagerly. Then she made them lie down and she sang a long lullaby in Kreyòl from deep in her throat.

After they were asleep, she covered the windows and put shreds of cloth and tissue paper into the cracks of the doors. The room was very dark and very quiet. Even the traffic in the street seemed to vanish as night fell and the soft breathing of the little girls filled the room. Georgette sang again, more softly, rocking herself on the floor with her eyes closed. She hoped they would sleep for a long time, until tomorrow night, until after this thing had passed, this meeting of sun and moon and earth. She wanted to sleep too, so she pressed more pills between the spoons and mixed it with more banana and ate it just as eagerly as the children had eaten theirs. She stretched out with them there, holding Annette closest to her, and fell asleep.

It was impossible to know what time it was when she woke. The room was dark and quiet, even more quiet than before. She waited and listened for a sound in the night. Surely it must be night, unless it was happening now, that magic darkness, that stinging light outside the door, trying to get through the cloth coverings and steal her away from her little daughters. She felt them next to her, sleeping, only they were so quiet, so still. She froze in the darkness and listened. Not a sound, not even the soft breathing that had been there after she finished the lullaby and their sleep filled the room.

Georgette's hand felt each head in the darkness. She could tell them apart, simply by touch. Sophie's hairline was lower and her ears close to her head. Jacqueline had more hair. And Annette, the smallest, had Hugo's fine boney features. She would be the most beautiful, one day, with sharp cheekbones and long arms and legs. Georgette's hands felt these differences, but as she touched them, terror traveled through her fingers straight into her heart, flashing like light sneaking around the moon in a ring of fire. No breathing. No movement. Each head was cool to the touch. Each mouth had a little trace of dried foam around it. Georgette sat up swiftly and straight, covering her face with both hands. When she let out a scream it woke Auntie in her soft bed, and in that house they knew the Devil himself had come and stolen the light right out of their hearts. After that day, nothing remained but darkness and the memory of three little girls playing beneath the almond tree.

Waiting for Love

mercredi

The island came into view on the left side of the plane, careening toward her like a giant moth, dull and velvet in a haze of shadows. She already knew of the villages, of lush banana fields and meandering rivers. In his letters, he had described walks along the canals and endless views from mountain paths. But coming at it like this, all of that was hidden deep inside the dark island below. From here, there was nothing to see but a large, sprawling city tossed out of a sack onto the mountainside. Port-au-Prince.

Pushing through a gust of heat toward the immigration desk, she scanned the crowd for his face. He was not expected and so she was not surprised at his absence. She would to go to the hotel and make herself comfortable, as they agreed. "I will come there. I will find you," he said. He wanted her to enjoy the veranda. Swim. Relax. Have a drink. "I will find you, dear Julie." It was a promise.

She smiled, recalling his words, repeating them to herself. *"Je te promis, ma chère Julie."*

She felt in her shoulder sack for the passport she hadn't used in five years and grazed the smooth stack of letters, two dozen of them, written in the past six months since their first meeting in Boston. She loved the blue paper, weightless as butterfly wings, and his wire-like handwriting, a mingling of French, Krèyol, and misspelled English. She treasured the rough sketches of plants he often included to illustrate his ideas. He believed there was a way to develop

Haiti's economy through agricultural resources. "Why they say we so poor?! We have so much!" Peanuts. Green-skinned oranges. Bananas. Vanilla beans. Rum! He was a large man with large ideas; muscular and dark-skinned. "Blueblack," she said, when she described him to a friend.

She found a taxi and locked the door. He had prepared her for thick traffic and teeming heat. The car climbed narrow, pitted streets past makeshift stands of soft drinks stagnating in glass bottles. A woman holding a baby wrapped in rags ran after the taxi, wailing. A wild-eyed boy on a bicycle shot out of an alley. Then, suddenly, the car lurched forward through an open gate into what seemed to be the Garden of Eden. A sign on the gate read: *Bienvenue Voyageurs.* Inside, the driveway of the hotel encircled a small sculpture garden with a fountain at the center and a cluster of stone snakes streaming with water. Shoots of palm and sheltering mango trees touched overhead in a deep green canopy. The pink and white building with a long veranda resembled a doll's house inserted in a thicket of tropical foliage. As she climbed the stone stairs, Julia could see the swimming pool in the far corner of the property, half hidden by an explosion of mimosa. When she entered the lobby with its cocktail bar and ceiling fans, she understood why this place had become a base camp and sanctuary for Americans and Europeans.

"Julia Stern, from Boston. I have a reservation."

"*Bienvenue Madame.*" The receptionist's skin was dark and shiny, like the polished mahogany wall behind her. She spoke in a hushed voice. "Jean will show you to your room."

In fact, it was a suite of three rooms situated on the left corner of the building connected to a long balcony echoing the length of the veranda below. White wicker furniture was arranged around a glass coffee table and, off to the side, a low bench held stacks of outdated American magazines. The balcony itself was eye-level with the tops of coconut palms and city roof tops gleaming in afternoon sunlight. The view stretched for miles, past the slums and the harbor where the sea glittered silently in the heat of the day.

Julia watched the city for a moment, like a bird on a branch. Then, shifting her gaze, she noticed the most startling sight of all, a canopy bed at the opposite end of the balcony shrouded in mosquito netting. She instantly imagined him there; both of them suspended in time, adored and adoring. She felt her neck change color. They had never touched, unless an earnest hug and rushed farewell kisses counted. "Write to me! I'll answer every letter, I promise!" Amazingly, they had come to love each other through letters and their love would be expressed soon. In this room. Of this, she was certain.

She crawled onto the bed, facing the panoramic view of the city and the sea. The entire country seemed to float before her eyes from this magical perch. She dragged her backpack onto the bed and felt deep inside for the letters. Precious letters. Beloved letters. She would read them again right now, even though she knew them by heart.

jeudi

She awoke with a jolt to the sound of a bird screaming like a woman. Pearl-colored light filtered through the gauze of the mosquito net. Her sense of time was lost in a dream. She must have fallen asleep but how long ago? What day was it? And where was Charlot?

Something was whining in her left ear, the high-pitched singing of a mosquito, that carrier of sickness. Charlot had warned her to take anti-malaria pills, to bring insect repellent, and to wear long-sleeved clothing at all times, especially in the city. She got up and went to the bathroom to find her small bottle of mosquito repellent and stepped on something sharp. Bees on the floor. Drowsy, drunken bees. She wrapped her head in a towel and slapped at them with a shoe, sending most of the survivors out of the open window. She slapped another bee to death, sprayed another with toxic repellent, and decided to go downstairs for breakfast.

All the tables on the porch were occupied by black couples, except for the small one near the stairs where a man dressed in blue jeans and a plaid shirt sat alone. He looked up at her, heavy-lidded, and beckoned with his hand as if they knew each other. "So what's the deal here? The cold stuff is free but if you want a few fried eggs order off the menu? Is that the way it works?"

Julia glanced over the one-page menu. "You're right. The fruit and bread over there come with the room."

"Well, I need a helluva a lot more than that to get started. Guess it's the *jambon omelette* for me. By the way, I'm Marvin Hopkins. From North Carolina."

"Julia Stern." She went to the buffet, returning with a wedge of green melon, three bananas, and a slice of bread.

Marvin helped himself to one of the bananas. "So, aren't you going to ask: What are you doing in Haiti? Well, hell, I'll tell you anyway. I'm an art dealer. My thing is called Outsider Art. Some people call it Contemporary Folk Art or Primitive Art. Different people call it different things. But whatever you call it, you can't fake it. Only genuine people who've escaped the mess of the modern world can make the stuff."

A waiter in a white jacket appeared with a pot of hot coffee and a bowl of sugar. "And then there's Haitian Art, which is in a class by itself. Some of the same people like it.

Right up there with the Sistine Chapel for some folks. No bullshit. So, I thought, what the hell. It's not that far to go. Might as well get my ass down here and see for myself. That was three years ago." He gulped the last chunk of banana.

Julia smiled, stirring her coffee.

"First couple of trips I came down with a guy from Miami who knew the ropes. He thought he'd broken me in but, hell, I still don't understand the place. All screwed up, but they make some damn good art. Lousy food, sick kids, too damn hot, but good art. So how about you?"

"What about me?"

"Everybody has a mission." He leaned forward as if to divulge a secret, "A *raison d'être*, as they say in French. But hey, don't speak French to me. I got a 'D' when I took it in high school." He peeled another banana, watching her with small brown eyes and a ruddy face that ended ambiguously in a gray, speckled beard.

"I'm a journalist from Boston. I cover environmental issues, mainly, agriculture, soil erosion, that sort of thing. But I'm not here to write an article."

"Got friends here?"

"Not exactly."

He leaned forward. His cheeks were pink beneath the sparse hair of his beard. "A boyfriend?"

She laughed nervously and turned to watch two boys in swimsuits dash from the lobby down the stairs of the veranda towards the pool. "I met someone at a conference on international agricultural trade. I guess you'd say he's my boyfriend." She felt her face grow hot and reached for a glass of water then smiled, regaining her confidence. "A wonderful man. A Haitian."

"A black guy?" He stopped eating for a moment and Stared, open-mouthed.

"That was six months ago and I'm here now to spend a week seeing the country. He's due here any time. Any minute, actually."

Marvin had helped himself to a slice of bread and covered it with a citrine-colored liquid spooned from a mason jar. "Guess this slop is what they use for jelly. So, what's he do for a living, this friend of yours?"

"Agriculture."

"And he knows you're here, waiting for him?"

"Of course he does. Of course." Suddenly, the whole thing sounded absurd, even to her. "He's been delayed, that's all. He warned me that things might not run smoothly."

"Well that's a god-damned understatement. Are you gonna eat that banana? And do you speak French?"

"Help yourself. And yes I do."

"Okay. So while you're waiting why don't you come out of the padded walls of paradise for a few hours and join me on a wild goose chase. There's an old man who makes sequined Vodou bottles right around the corner. Cool as shit. And there's a French guy with a house full of art. I gotta get over there today or tomorrow."

"Oh, no, I couldn't." Her back straightened as she took a gulp off water. "You see I'm expecting him any time now. I'm sure he's on his way and I couldn't—not be here." He studied her face as it flushed uncontrollably. The strange field between them was interrupted by the mist of a steaming omelette. "He *expects* me to be here. But thanks anyway."

Marvin attacked the omelette with a spoon, finished it quickly, and stood up. Beads of sweat appeared on his forehead from the exertion of eating. "Well, I hope he shows up. Anyway, you have a good day now." Before she could reply he was gone.

Julia sat a while, drinking coffee and orange juice, thinking of her purpose here, her un-humanitarian "mission." It was a romantic quest. That's what it was, but was it foolish? Did it matter less than art or peanut butter production? The letters were real; that much she was sure of. And didn't love deserve a chance?

A swim would kill time and cure the sadness taking root inside of her like a fragile seed. Sun and water. Maybe even a silent prayer. Julia Stern had been praying underwater since childhood, wet and muffled in the silence of deep, all-encompassing water. She ordered more coffee that took ten minutes to arrive. Time moved more slowly here. She had to learn to feel things at a different pace. He was probably on his way. They would laugh about it later, how she spent the entire morning feeling sad and anxious. How she swam like fish without fins, praying for him to come.

By the time she finished her meal and changed into a swimsuit the pool was empty. She allowed the water to draw her in. Six feet. Ten feet. Twelve. The heat of the morning sun through depths of water felt good on her back. She went under then brought her head up quickly, making a sleek cap of her auburn hair. Rising through the film of water and white heat, she saw his thick neck and broad back as she lifted herself out of the pool, heart pounding. A voice in her head called his name. *Charlot. You have come. You have found me.* A car horn sounded in the street and a deep-voiced woman called out from the kitchen of the hotel. Life was going on but *Charlot, you have come.* But then she saw the other woman with that man, and then a child. And when he turned she could see that he was too old to be Charlot. She fell back and floated, face up, eyes closed, thinking that she might float there forever, waiting for love.

vendredi

Julia awoke the next morning to the same screeching bird and the same pale light rising over the city. She had folded the letters full of promises the night before and returned them to their envelopes. The words were etched in her mind; the sentence where he said his thoughts of her were carried like a secret pain beneath his skin. He said he longed for her and yet feared the power of her touch, which he could sense in her bold handwriting. He traced his hand on a sheet of paper, asking her to do the same. It was a few weeks after that when he called and left a message crackling with static. There was no way to call him back.

The bathroom smelled of insecticide now. The bees were gone, though a few lay dead on the floor. She poured filtered water from a pitcher into the sink and brought handfuls of it up to her face. When she encountered her face in the mirror she saw a surprising puffiness around the eyes, a slightly swollen jaw. Could she be ill? She stepped into a tepid shower, remembering their last hug and those small, hurried kisses. It had not been clear at the time if they were simply awkward expressions of affection or something more. A lingering embrace, then "butterfly" kisses across the face. She closed her eyes, trying to remember. They had barely touched at all, but as she felt that touch slipping away, that memory becoming distant, something tore at her heart. In the shower, she wept and whispered his name. A slow bee, half dead, crawled along the soap dish, slipped on the edge, and toppled into the water like a drunken fool.

That afternoon, she climbed a steep hill in a nearby neighborhood with Marvin panting next to her, his face streaming with sweat that disappeared into his beard. They walked in the cement gutter because the edge of the street captured sharp planes of shade from the houses. At the top of the hill, just past the convent, Marvin stopped at an iron gate and pulled on a rope attached to a heavy bell. A large woman opened the gate and led them silently along a row of golden hibiscus to the back door. There, on the step, a boy with a blank expression was softly patting drums. Suddenly, a white man in his fifties with a European accent burst through the door. "Marvin! Bonjour! And who's this? Don't tell me it's your wife?!"

"Not a chance. Julia just came along for the ride. Forgot to tell her she might have a heart attack before she got here. Julia, Alain DuBois at your service, finder and financier of fine Haitian paintings."

"He means I give the young men art supplies now and then—"

"In return for half of what they produce!"

Alain laughed, throwing his head back. "Sometimes it's charity. Sometimes it's an investment. Come in, I'll show you what I mean."

Inside, a narrow hallway led to a salon with high ceilings and shuttered French doors. Deep green walls were hung with paintings, floor to ceiling. Stacks of paintings separated by sheets of cardboard leaned against every wall. In the corner, four Louis XVI chairs faced an empty easel, their worn upholstery sagging with the weight of time. Alain Dubois moved quickly to place a canvas there for viewing.

"Sit down, sit down, *je vous en prie*, I will show you the best of the best!" They sat in the fragile, elegant chairs as he presented an unframed image of a misty jungle where a group of women bathed behind the curtain of a waterfall. Overhead, in the blue-green landscape and azure sky, trees were heavy with exaggerated fruit, pineapple and mangoes, coconuts and bananas. Above that a goddess-like face emerged in the upper right corner, where soft clouds spelled *ERZULIE* in vaporous puffs.

"Holy shit," Marvin said.

"What does it mean?" Julia asked.

"It's the Goddess of Femininity and Fertility, my favorite of the Vodou Pantheon."

"This is Vodou? But it's beautiful!"

Alain smiled. "Ah, *chère Madame*! You suffer from that old American fear! You think Vodou is some sort of evil terror! Ha! Do you realize what power this gives us here?! In Haiti, Vodou is life! Life and death! It is *everything*!"

Julia studied the painting. There were no men in the picture, only women, water, plants, and sky; large women with rapturous faces, half-dressed, long-limbed, some of them swollen with unborn children. Their arms waved in the air, obscured by blue mist.

Julia stared at the strange canvas. "It's like a dream," she said.

"It IS a dream," Alain said. "You like this one?" Alain looked directly at Marvin. "Only eight hundred dollars, for you. Today"

"Show me more."

Alain brought out a small, dark canvas centered with a cross and flames. It was a mystical painting decorated with a border of disembodied feet and clapping hands. An eye at the top glared like a jewel. A top hat floated above the eye.

"*Baron Samedi*," said Marvin.

"The dance of death, of course."

"And who is *Baron Samedi*?" Julie stared at the picture.

Marvin held out his hand to Alain as if to say, *you explain*. The expert obliged. "*Baron Samedi* is the spirit you would appeal to for the ordinary problems of daily life. He is also the leader of the *Gédé*, the spirits of the dead. It is very

important in Haiti to stay on good terms with the dead."
Alain laughed. "They can make your life miserable!"

"How much?"

"Six hundred!"

Marvin smiled. "I'll take it."

"And not other?"

"I'll take both."

To celebrate the transaction, Alain brought out a
bottle of rum and three plastic cups. "To art," he said, raising
the bottle, "and to my good friends."

"Who will buy them?" Julia asked later, as they
descended the hill.

"A professor, probably, an anthropologist."

"I wish I could buy them," she said off-handedly.

Marvin stopped in his tracks like an animal. "Do you
want to go back? He has more. He always has more, though I
betcha these are the best."

"No, that's alright. I like it, that's all." She shrugged
her shoulders.

They continued down the hill, heads bent against the
ferocious sun. "I told you, didn't I? Great stuff down here.
Cool as shit."

* * *

Julia showered before dinner, imagining herself in the cool
waterfall of the painting, her body full as a ripe melon. There
was no message for her at the front desk. No call. No
Charlot. She dried herself slowly, replaying his words in her
mind. *I will come there. I will find you.* Then she heard something;
quick steps coming toward her room. Up the stairs, down the
hall, a key wiggling in the lock. At last, he had come. Of
course, of course. How could she ever have doubted him?

Charlot, my love! She quickly twisted the towel above her breasts, rushing to the door, tears rising in her throat, opening the tall wooden door so quickly that the man holding the key fell forward.

"Oh dear. I beg your pardon." The fine-featured stranger spoke in a monotone British accent, holding his key in the air. "I was looking for Room Number Two." He was lean and tanned, dressed in khaki, and peering at her through wire glasses.

"This is Two and a Half." She lowered her eyes and stepped behind the door.

"Terribly sorry. Really."

Julia closed the door slowly and stood for a long time with eyes shut, bare back to the heavy wooden door, feeling a strange heat rising inside. She pressed her head against the door as something emptied from her limbs like hot water poured out of a jug. How could it have come to this? And what would she say on her return to Boston? Maybe no one would ask. Most of them assumed she was visiting an old friend in Miami. Maybe no one cared. Maybe they, too, had stood naked and alone somewhere like this. Only a couple of close friends had ever even heard of Charlot. "Blueblack," she told them, enjoying the small *frisson* of surprise.

"I suppose we're supposed to be too PC to care about race," Barbara had said with an ironic smile.

"Yes. I suppose so."

"But you can't really ignore it, can you?"

"I think I love him."

Julia sighed deeply. It was pathetic, that's what it was. A pathetic hope, a *rendez-vous* with a man who decided to jilt her. But what if he *hadn't* jilted her? What if he was injured or ill or killed by a bullet? What if they were like Cary Grant and Deborah Kerr in that old movie, so close to the moment of truth and yet kept apart by tragedy, by chance? Her body stiffened, then went slack with resignation. Suddenly, her hands covered her face in a gesture that released the green towel from her naked body. It gathered like moss around her damp, bare feet.

What a risk. And yet if it had worked out—if only it had worked out, she might have returned with a deep, enviable happiness. Then, *if it had worked out*, their love would have been worth everything. Under those circumstances, those who heard about it would marvel at their confidence, their deep faith in the power of love. They would tell their fairy tale again and again, reliving their sense of wonder at finding each other so unexpectedly. But the alternative. Oh hell. The alternative was the indignity of standing here at age 38, alone in a strange country, naked, exhausted, and humiliated like the unwanted children peddling overripe bananas in the street.

"I *do* believe in the power of love," she whispered. Even if it was cruel. Even if it stripped the unloved and destroyed the unlucky.

Julia looked out at a thousand sheet-metal rooftops. The sun was low and sinking. Night would soon engulf the hotel and she would descend to the lobby to immerse herself in alcohol and murmuring voices. Marvin might be down there sipping a Mai Tai. The British man in wire glasses might say hello or offer to buy her a gin and tonic. Later, she would sleep in the canopy bed, imagining Charlot's hands on her body, the shape of them familiar from his tracing, the color deep and glossy like the skin of an eggplant except for pale palms. His spirit would lift her up and send her forward, into the night, into the trees like a bird screaming with joy.

Such dreams would stay with her for a long time. Years later, after returning to Boston and winning awards for socially responsible journalism she would relive these nights without Charlot in the darkness. Long after she stopped believing, after his features had softened in memory, even then she would find herself returning to a strange sensation that was his unknown touch; unknown, unseen, untasted. A memory she could only imagine.

It would start with a thin, rolling sensation as she drifted off to sleep, like a ballpoint pen writing along the length of her arms and legs. This hand-writing traveled slowly down to her ankles and up across her sunburnt shoulders. She learned to watch the line of it through the telescope of memory and desire, smiling as he covered her with writing: *je t'aime . . . tu me manques ... nous sommes toujours emsemble, mon amour. . . I will find you.* He rolled her over and wrote in a long, continuous line along her spine, conquering her with words as he trussed her body with scribbles, dragging a pen around and around. In those dreams her body became a landscape of his handwriting, a blank page filled with thoughts of love. Sooner or later, a bird screamed or a siren wailed in the distance of the city and her eyes snapped open to the shock of a new day.

"Charlot," she mumbled. "Come back."

samedi

Just before the car arrived to take her to the airport, she walked down the steps to the pool past a colossal concrete lizard and the fountain full of stone-carved snakes. There was nothing to wait for anymore, nothing to wish for, nothing to regret. Even if he came tonight or tomorrow, it would not matter now. Every love has its moment and their moment had passed. She would destroy the letters later. She would have to destroy the letters, that was clear, but she wanted to think about how to do it. She wanted to think about that very carefully.

Waiting for the car, Julia stepped back and watched circles of light moving on the surface of the chlorinated water. Each circle seemed to melt into another, forming a web of floating light like a fisherman's net cast wide. She remembered the woman who had plunged into that web, crawled into the silence beneath it and prayed. She remembered the faith she had arrived with, the faith that had carried her into the deep end. She remembered herself gently, as one recalls a last good-bye, the final smile, a hand waving from a car. Words rushed to the surface and stopped. There was so much to say that would never be said; so much that could not be written about the love contained in those letters. The taxi arrived late, horn honking. She hurried toward it, eager to leave this place. There was no reason to stay here now and no choice but to leave some part of her self behind—swimming in hope, caught in the net, drowning in imaginary love.

Evening Prayer

Nuns inhabit the city like pigeons, their white and gray dresses billowing as they walk, habits pulled tight around serene faces. The good sisters of Port-au-Prince come from all over the world, but mostly from America and Europe, sometimes staying for a very long time. They love the children. In the children's faces they see the light of Christ, the hope of the world. In the orphanages, in the hospitals, in the school yards you see them with the children, teaching and smiling, tossing a ball. They sing and tell stories. They listen to small voices and hold small hands. Every day, the good sisters rise in the heat of the morning and begin their daily life of prayer and service. From the safety of their convents and churches, bells clamor over city traffic, over human conversation, calling the sisters to daily offices of prayer and Holy Eucharist. Every evening they bow their heads in thanks for another day, another chance to do God's work. At night, after a simple meal and meditation, they remove their plain clothes and rest in unadorned rooms, comforted by a fierce faith and the ever-present hope of tomorrow.

Sister Gloria hurried down the hall toward the bell tower. It was impolite to run inside the convent, but she had been running all day and was barely aware of her pace. At the end of the hall she swung around to the right and encountered Sister Rachel. The old woman took in a quick breath. Her hand flew to her chest like a fan.

"I'm sorry, Sister Rachel. So very sorry." There were no other words spoken as each woman continued in opposite directions.

Sister Gloria spoke to herself as she moved more steadily toward the tower. I must learn to calm down. I must learn to do all that is expected of me without rushing. I must pray for serenity and grace and strength and gentleness and kindness and compassion and intelligence. Dear God, there were so many things to pray for, so many ways for God to work through her small being. It was hard to discern God's Will for such an imperfect servant. In four years of living close to God she still wasn't sure what He wanted of her and sometimes felt that so little had been accomplished. As a postulant she had imagined she would be more graceful by now. As a novice she had learned it would take rigorous discipline and devotion over a long period of time. And after her first profession of vows last year she discovered the possibility that she might never become all that God had dreamed for her, no matter how hard she tried.

"God will guide you," Sister Clare had said with a smile. "Pray for His guidance and He will work through you in amazing ways." Sister Clare's hand against her cheekbone felt soft and strong at the same time.

And so she had prayed and so He had given her a small talent to help the children at the convent school. It came quite unexpectedly one afternoon when a group of little girls was waiting just outside the convent wall, enjoying the shade of a tall tree. They were leaning against the tree when Sister Gloria started to tell them a story. The story came from nowhere but suddenly it was on her lips. There was a giant melon and an old man who wanted to give the melon to his wife as a present. He tried to ride a bicycle with the melon but couldn't. He tried to walk with the melon on his head but couldn't. He even jumped off a building with the melon, trying to fly and fell on his back, but managed to keep the melon in one piece by catching it and holding it tight like a child. The girls laughed when he caught the melon just in time and rolled with it into the road.

But this fall gave him an idea, Sister Gloria explained, because this fall was truly a gift from God. You see, when he was up on the roof the man prayed for God's help and God told him to roll the melon home by showing him how to roll himself right into the road. After he got up and saw that the melon was whole, he tapped it with his foot and to his surprise, the melon rolled all the way down the road to his village and right up the steps of his house and broke into two, perfect halves so his wife didn't even have to cut it. That was a good thing too, Sister Gloria explained, because his wife didn't have a knife big enough to cut that melon. And even more to his surprise a beautiful orange bird flew out of the melon and gave his wife a kiss which made her very happy. The girls laughed in the sunshine and from that day on remembered Sister Gloria's Tale of the Magic Melon.

"God has given you a talent," said Sister Clare. "He will show you how to use it."

And so He did. For without even trying the young nun made up more stories about fruits and flowers, birds and leaves, rocks that turned into loaves of bread and lizards who gobbled up gold earrings and whispered in the ears of rich ladies. This small talent is the best thing that God has given me, Sister Gloria thought as she walked past a long row of windows that looked out across the city. The rooftops were dull in the cloudy light and the palm trees swayed like feathers in the wind. It was surely going to rain any minute and that would mean traffic accidents and break-ins in the neighborhood. The rain was so thick and furious here that it always presented a fine opportunity for thieves. She wondered if Sister Margaret had remembered to lock the gate.

Sister Gloria's mind wandered as she made her way up the narrow steps to the bell tower. She imagined her father in Miami bent over his desk at the insurance company. She held an image of her mother in front of her for a long moment, a petite woman on her knees in the garden, cutting roses for the kitchen table. Somewhere else, her brother was teaching a class and her niece and nephew were playing in a sprinkler. She sighed, remembering how alarmed they all had been by her decision to join the order and commit herself to a life in the church. Dad wept and turned away when she left but Mother smiled bravely and said, "You'll make a wonderful life for yourself. I know you will."

But had she? Was she making a life of any kind? Making up stories in the schoolyard was fun but it was such a small thing. The heat made her tired. The work was endless as each day blended into the next. Bad things were always happening and it seemed she could do so little to help. She quickened her pace again, unaware, and wondered why God had chosen to do his best work through other people. It was a selfish thought, but there it was. She prayed to be better, to be worthy, to be a ray of God's light in the world.

At the top of the steps Sister Gloria entered a small, open bell tower where the heavy bell hung with a thick rope dangling next to it. Rain was falling like soft kisses and cool breezes pushed her white habit away from her face. Her eyes were large and her cheeks flushed with the effort of climbing those steps. It was 5:15. Just enough time to ring the bell and give the sisters fifteen minutes to come to Evening Prayer. They would come from the kitchen and the church and their offices in the convent school. There might be a few sisters outside the convent walls, walking in the neighborhood to check in on sick people or new mothers. They would come too, summoned by the deep, brassy call of the bell. The rain fell harder as Sister Gloria grabbed the rope. In the street she heard shouts but the rain and wind made noise in the tall trees, drowning out voices.

As she pulled on the rope she heard a popping noise and had a flash memory of television movies and popcorn with Mother on Friday nights, just the two of them, while Dad and Allen went to a ball game. "You'll make a wonderful life for yourself," Mother had said. It was a comfort to remember those words as her hands twisted around the rope. In her own way, Mother was a person of faith because she believed in her children, in her husband, in her world, even though she didn't go to church regularly. Sister Gloria smiled to herself as she formed that thought, thanking God for that awareness of her own, little mother in the garden.

The bell was clanging now, filling the air with a loud, metallic beauty. If that sound was a color, it would be blue, she thought. Deep, watery blue like the ocean. She was grateful for the strength to do this work, to be the bell ringer, the one who called everyone together at the end of the day. Perhaps this was what God wanted most of her. She was young and strong, in spite of her small size. Maybe this was the kind of strength He needed most, here and now in this troubled place. Maybe the sound of the bell gave people hope and confidence, for what was the point of such daily routines if not reassurance of God's presence?

Beneath the sound of the bell there was a car horn honking and a rip of screeching rubber. The hollow ringing of the bell seemed to contain those sounds along with the popping noise and the hard spatter of rain. Cars and popcorn. Rain. Church bells pouring over rooftops like a shower of coins. She could see dark, wet faces hurrying in the road, running to escape the torrent of rainwater that would soon consume and conceal everything. Sister Gloria felt a strange joy beating in her chest and sent silent prayers into the air, looking up as if she could see them, as if they were birds scattering from a tree. She tugged at the rope and smiled at the wild noise of the moment then turned her head toward the street. The plane of her left cheek glistened with moisture, flat and rose-colored. People were running and shouting. A man waved a dark object in the air. A gun. A gun waving in the air. She could see the gun through the trees, pointing at her face like a camera. There was a moment of confusion. Should she smile or scream? Sister Gloria opened her mouth to pray aloud, to scream her prayer, to plead with God. The man with the gun heard the scream, but too late. Who was screaming? Who? Who? The gun exploded and she fell quickly, her hand sliding away from the rope like a lizard slinking out of sight.

They would find her body later, following the ribbon of blood up the stairs to the bell tower. The man with the gun would be gone by then, vanished into the rain-drenched city, riding a tap-tap or smoking cigarettes at a small table where card games went on all night. No one would remember his face or name. No one would speak about it.

Later, the good sisters would say that Sister Gloria died with her protector. They would pray for understanding and forgiveness, determined to accept God's will, His choice for her, His dream. Her family would listen as the good sisters described the dark clouds gathering overhead and feel the echo of the bell as it filled the air with dark music, swinging with resounding strength. They could still smell fury in the trees as they told the story of that day, remembering how quickly the ringing stopped.

It was a rainy day last summer, "just before Evening Prayer." They repeated that phrase several times, as if it held the key to God's mystery. "The Lord knew it was coming," they told each other. "He knows tomorrow before we can imagine it."

There was a silence in the room, a clearing of someone's throat. "Sister Gloria will always be here, calling others to pray." These were the soft-spoken words of the Mother Superior as she tried to comfort the father who left the room. The mother remained seated, eyes glistening, head bobbing nervously in an effort to understand what has happened here. She wanted to ask about an investigation but could not find the words. She wondered about justice outside the walls of the convent. "It is a small legacy," they tell her, "a small sound in a big city, but to think of the bell as Sister's Gloria's voice, calling us to prayer, is a blessing for all of us."

The Artist's Wife

Everyone likes to paint, but everyone is not an artist. In Port-au-Prince they sell pictures on street corners, in the airport shops, at hotels, and door-to-door in places where tourists and missionaries go. Some artists have apprentices, groups of boys who help them finish their paintings faster, making more to sell. Gallery owners, websites, even cab drivers sell paintings. It is always the same subject, the deep green countryside where Black Madonnas carry fruit in round baskets balanced on their heads, fruit that echoes the curves of their bodies. Leaves and flowers, ripe fruit, and smooth-skinned women. It is the artists who find beauty in this place, hunting it down, capturing it, no matter how elusive. Haitian artists find customers in America, so Americans believe they have the best collections of Haitian art. But that is a lie because the true treasure is always hidden, never leaving the realm of its creation.

A few people whispered as Lilliane Hippolyte crossed the hot tarmac in Port-au-Prince and swayed into the crowded aisle of the plane. She was a large and dignified Haitian woman, like an African Queen with hair arranged upward and earrings made of fake gold dangling the length of her thick neck. She wore a cotton jacket and a long floral dress. Isn't she someone famous, they whispered as she lumbered forward. Is it her, the mother of the president or maybe the wife of that artist who died last year, dropped dead in broad daylight didn't he? That's it. She is the wife of Max Hippolyte. They remembered seeing her photograph at his funeral in *Le Nouvelliste.*

Lilliane felt conspicuous in such a small place. She pushed her cross-tied bundle under the seat and squeezed in next to the window. She had never been on an airplane before and never traveled to America. Already it felt like a bad idea, even though the cost was covered by the university in Boston where eight of Max's paintings would be on exhibit for a month. A young woman with a coconut-colored baby stood in the aisle studying seat numbers then moved on. A white man in a tee-shirt that said NO PAIN, NO GAIN moved in quickly and dropped into the seat next to her. *"Bonjour,"* he said grudgingly. His eyes were pulled forward, pensive and frowning.

Lilliane stared out the window at the concrete buildings and hazy sky. It was a hot day and she had been awake since 5 a.m. The house was locked, the plants were watered. Monsieur Jo-Jo would come and feed the birds tomorrow, two old parrots named Lola and Maurice after Max's grandparents. Everything was done so she might as well go, she told herself as she walked down the hill at dawn to catch a tap-tap. But now that she had gotten this far, she wanted to turn back. Her lungs filled slowly as she looked toward the door. A white girl in a neat, navy blue suit was pulling the latch, smiling at the wall with painted lips. "Prepare for take-off," a voice said as another girl with a bright smile leaned across the white man and asked Lilliane to fasten her seatbelt. The belt was too tight but she obliged. The young man put a headset over his ears and closed his eyes as the plane began to move.

Ever since the young American professor had contacted her and come all the way to Haiti last January, Lilliane had lived behind a veil of dread and excitement. They wanted to honor Max Hippolyte with a special exhibition of Haitian art, he said, sitting in the yard with a fine leather satchel leaning against his foot. There would also be work by Haitian-American artists living and working in Boston and a special wall devoted to Max Hippolyte. "The *diaspora*, you know," he said, enunciating the word, *diaspora* as if it were a secret. Many people in Boston owned paintings by Max Hippolyte. Did she have any others that she might loan to this exhibition?

Lilliane laughed aloud as she recalled that question in his first letter. Did she have any others? Only every inch of every wall, she wanted to say, though she knew that every picture she owned was not her husband's best work. But so what? She was not a critic or a dealer or a collector. She was the artist's wife and she loved each painting because each one held a memory, a moment, a vivid image of Max working in the garden or in the studio. She remembered his paint-stained hands and the little bits of speckled cloth that used to pile up in the studio. She remembered the smell of paint and the stark excitement of prepared canvas—stretched taut and carefully primed—before he went to work on it. Do you have any others? *Mon Seigneur*! She had a few hundred and most of them had been photographed and made into slides. Would that interest the young American professor? She wrote back with a proud heart.

Dr. Gabriel Jones came quickly, flying to Port-au-Prince from Boston with his leather satchel, a tape recorder, a digital camera, and an envelope filled with letters of introduction, including one from the Haitian Consulate and another from a dean at the famous university. This young man was well-prepared, she thought, as they sat for an hour in the small garden drinking limeade before she let him into the house. His eyes told her that he was sincere, that he respected art. He followed her room to room, looking up and down, admiring the paintings that hung in the shadows from floor to ceiling in wooden frames Max made himself. "This is beautiful," he said with a broad smile. "Beautiful." She noticed that he wasn't looking at any particular painting when he said that.

Later he asked, "How did he work? Inside the studio from memory? Or *en plein air*?" He spoke good French and wanted to know everything. He asked if he could turn on the tape recorder and she nodded. Could he take a few photos? When did Max begin to paint? How did he work? Which series was his own personal favorite? He asked a lot of questions but they were all easy to answer. Then he asked her if she would like to come to America and attend the reception for the exhibition in September. He thought he could get funds to cover her travel and her stay in Boston. Would she like to stay at his house for or three days, or would she prefer a hotel? Lilliane shrugged her shoulders as she straightened a painting in the tiny hallway. "You have been to my home. I would like to come to your home," she said. Dr. Jones smiled at that and said he would take care of everything.

After he left, she stood in the main room of the house and watched golden light streaming across Max's canvases, turning his greens and purples into sparkling jewels. She loved the way the house came to life at this hour of the day, the dance of light and shade on the polished wood furniture, the scuttle of Lola and Maurice in their cage in the kitchen. She walked into the bedroom where the flickering light continued to dart through wooden slats. Her favorite paintings were here, in this small space protected by the carved mahogany shutters Max had made so they could sleep or make love at any hour of the day. His only self-portrait hung next to the bureau on a narrow slice of wall.

"You coming to be a famous man," she said quietly to the self-portrait. "I'll do for you what I said I would. I'll help you out, you know I will." She smiled at the deep-set eyes that stared back at her with the ribbon-like curl of green leaves behind him; the silvery light made his head look hard and shiny like a bed post. "I'll always do it," she said, "until God sends me someplace else."

Soon after his visit, Dr. Jones sent her a plane ticket with a typed letter that told her how to get a visa to travel outside of Haiti. She didn't like the forms she had to fill out or the waiting rooms filled with young people and small children. It seemed that everyone wanted to travel outside of Haiti but no one looked happy about it. Besides, it was hard work finding the right office and getting the forms to the right person before the office closed for the day. Dr. Jones also sent her money to reproduce a careful selection of her slides and to cover the cost of mailing them to America. Then, a week before her departure, he sent forty American dollars in cash wrapped in several sheets of paper so she would have some money to use when she got to Miami.

"Everyone is very happy that you can come," he wrote. "I will introduce you at the reception as the artist's wife and you will be proud."

That was the first thing Dr. Jones said that she didn't like. Didn't he understand she was already proud to be the wife of Max Hippolyte? She had been proud to ride on his bicycle handlebars when they were still in school and she had been proud to be his lover under the trees along the beaches and be his bride and have his children and cook his food and keep his home. She didn't need any trip to America to be proud of her life as the wife of Max Hippolyte.

"Why do you do so much for him?" her sister asked a long time ago.

"He is a great artist," she replied. "You don't expect Michelangelo to take out the garbage, do you?"

Her sister shrieked with laughter at that remark and afterwards she always called her brother-in-law "Michelangelo." She found a picture of the Sistine Chapel in a magazine and gave it to Lilliane. It was a joke, but it was also a sign of respect.

* * *

The plane landed in Miami and everyone had to get out and walk a long way down two empty corridors and up steep flights of steps to a little booth where a man with a silver badge stamped travel documents. Then there was another long corridor with swinging aluminum doors and light fixtures floating on the low ceiling that gave out a flat, greenish light. Lilliane had never seen such a big building. After a long walk she came to a vast open area with food counters all around and electric signs that spelled out words like TACOS and PIZZA. People were sitting at round tables eating food out Styrofoam containers that most of them left on the table when they got up. She wanted to sit down and drink some coffee but she was afraid she would miss the next plane from Miami to Boston if she stopped moving. It wasn't clear where the plane was or how long it would take to get to it and find her seat.

She kept walking past the food counters and found herself in another long hallway that led to a pavilion with tall glass windows. There were shops, carts, and crowds of people in the pavilion and more round tables and Styrofoam cups and plastic boxes. Everyone seemed busy and in a hurry, so she tried to walk faster, trying to feel more like them. She put her bundle on her head to balance the weight and free up her arms. Then she found an airline desk and a place to sit until it was time for her flight. Her watch said two o'clock. The plane would leave at two thirty. She sighed and decided to sit right where she was until someone told her to get on the plane.

When the plane landed in Boston there was a loud bump and a whoosh of cold air. Lilliane was glad to see Dr. Jones when she came out into the waiting room. "A familiar face is a good thing," she said as they shook hands.

He was surprised she had made the journey with a single bundle and no checked baggage but seemed glad too. "That will save us some time," he said. "Friday traffic is always pretty bad here." They drove into the mouth of the city, through a dark tunnel and along a four-lane highway streaming with fast cars. The drive seemed to last a long while and Lilliane held her breath most of the way. Everything she saw was gray or blurred by speed. Finally, they left the highway and pulled into the driveway of a brick house surrounded by a dark green hedge.

Inside, Leslie Jones stood smiling as her husband introduced "the esteemed Lilliane Hippolyte, the artist's wife." Leslie was pale and flat-faced with thick black hair that she tucked behind her ears. She led Lilliane toward the back of the house to a private room with its own bathroom and a window that looked out on the back yard. It was a small yard, a square of dull grass with a neat hedge growing along one side. There were no birds or flowers or children in the yard. Lilliane wrinkled her nose and wondered why.

"You must be tired," Leslie said, "and we really should leave for the reception in an hour. So maybe you'd like to lie down. Or maybe you'd like to have some coffee, or a glass of juice." Lilliane looked at the young woman, not knowing what to say. Was it polite to arrive at someone's house and lie down before you even had a chance to talk? She didn't know.

"Well, why don't you freshen up and let me know," Leslie said, closing the door to the room. Lilliane did not know what it meant to "freshen up" so she stood at the window for a while, then went out and asked for a glass of water, still clutching her bundle. She decided to keep it with her, even though Leslie Jones tried to convince her to leave it behind.

* * *

The reception for the Haitian Art Exhibit Featuring the Work of Max Hippolyte took place in a spacious gallery at a university near the center of the city. The crowd was humming like a beehive when they entered, each face turning to watch as Leslie and Gabriel Jones guided Lilliane to the green wall with large red letters: Max Hippolyte 1934-2002. There were five other walls in the L-shaped gallery, each hung with tropical landscapes and close-up portraits of black faces and naked women, but the green wall was for Max alone. Lilliane stood in front of it and studied the pictures with blank eyes. This is not his best work, she thought, as she remembered the waterfalls and banana fields where he had first sketched these scenes. There were dark women with baskets balanced on their heads, donkeys and houses, banana groves and forests, but the eight paintings presented here seemed too small on this big wall and the room was too noisy to see them with a clear head. It is better to look at his work in the quiet of our house, she thought, as Dr. Jones led her to a machine that looked like a television set and flipped a switch.

The machine whirred as if it were breathing heavily, then made clicking sounds as images of Max's paintings flashed before her eyes. This is better work, she thought, but there was no texture to the surface of the machine so the pictures looked faraway and the colors seemed to melt in the hot light. Lilliane felt sad and turned away. It was as if Max's paintings had been chopped up and sent to America and fed to the machine. The leaves and flowers were in the wrong place, like rooster feathers on a goat, she thought.

"I'd like to sit down," she said softly, but she could see there was no stool or bench nearby. Dr. Jones gave his wife a worried look and sent someone out for a folding chair. The room was cold and everyone spoke in rapid English, a sound that reminded Lilliane of hands clapping. The women were thin and dressed in dark, short dresses. Most of the men were pale and scrubbed with pink, spongy faces. Others had beards and prickly moustaches and one, a student, wore his hair in long braids.

A chair appeared and Lilliane sat down across from the green wall with Max's name on it, the central picture reminding her of the mountains she knew as a child. Her feet hurt but she was afraid to remove her shoes. Leslie Jones vanished and returned with a cup of punch that tasted sour. Lilliane wanted to spit it out but there was nowhere to spit so she swallowed it quickly and coughed. Leslie came back again with a glass of water and a plate of food, small, hard triangles covered with salt. A few people stopped and said hello, but the black people she met seemed uncomfortable and the white people seemed to laugh at her behind sharp features. A young man with silver rings in his nose and eyebrows shook her hand and said he admired her husband's work. He said he was an artist too so she smiled at him.

After a while, no one seemed to notice her anymore. Gabriel and Leslie Jones were at the other end of the room surrounded with white people wearing expensive clothes. Lilliane was glad to be invisible for a while, though she was still hungry and wondered if anyone would be bringing out rice or meat. She remembered the avocados at home on the kitchen table and the half melon still in the refrigerator. She wondered if Monsieur Jo-Jo would help himself to a slice of that when he came to feed the old parrots. She hoped he would because otherwise the melon would spoil. It was hard to shop for one person after having a man around for years who was willing to eat everything in sight.

A new group of people arrived like a flock of birds. Lilliane watched Leslie grab their hands then stop to chat with a tall man in a suit. Suddenly, Lilliane couldn't stand it anymore. She stood up and hurried through the crowd, down the steps, and out into the street, cradling her round bundle. They would think she had gone off to find a toilette. That would give her some time. From the sidewalk, she could see the gallery glowing behind her and the green wall at one end of it. She walked briskly until she came to a busy intersection where she stood for a long time until a taxi cab stopped at the light and opened the door.

"I must get to the airport," she said. "I'm late."

The cab driver flipped a lever on his dash board and drove fast so Lilliane bounced up and down, like riding a horse down a path. She held tight to the vinyl arm rest and smiled broadly, glad to be going home. She would get back on the next plane and be home in time for sunrise in the garden.

***

After waiting a while in a long room with seats welded to the floor, a black man in a uniform told her she was in the wrong terminal. She followed him around a curved wall of mirrored glass that multiplied their images two hundred times. She removed her shoes and stuffed them into the bundle which she carried on her head until she found a sign she recognized.

"You can't change this ticket without an extra charge." It was another American girl in a navy blue suit.

"How much?"

"Seventy-five dollars. If you have a visa I can charge it for you."

Lilliane smiled, relieved, and reached into the pocket of her cloth coat for her travel documents. She placed her visa on the counter with a smile.

"No, I'm sorry, not that kind of visa. I mean a credit card. A VISA. Do you have a credit card?"

Lilliane looked puzzled.

"Anyway, there's no flight tonight. You'd have to wait until six o'clock in the morning. But I'd need a way to pay for the change."

"I have no way to pay," Lilliane said, staring passively at the girl.

"I see." The girl looked away, as if to search for help. "I'm sorry. You see, we have to go by the ticket you have. And it's for Monday at six o'clock in the morning."

"Monday morning at six o'clock," Lilliane echoed the words. "That will be fine."

She walked away from the girl without saying anything else. It was Friday night. Monday morning was a long way off, but the buildings had electricity and water fountains and plenty of toilettes. There was cheap food to eat too, like French fries and ice cream. The chairs were wide and padded and if she looked around, she figured she could find a place to stretch out. The rest of the time she would just walk around or look at American newspapers. It wouldn't be so bad. These airports are like towns, she told herself. People were walking along as if they were going to work. What was the difference? Once when they were young, she and Max lived on the beach for two weeks without a hotel room, sharing a hammock and waking at dawn to the sound of waves and gulls. Two days of living in a big modern airport didn't seem so bad. She settled into a chair and began to wait.

* * *

When Lilliane Hippolyte landed in Port-au-Prince on Monday evening, she took a cab to her house and paid the driver ten American dollars, the last of the money from Dr. Jones. The house was quiet on the outside, half-hidden in evening shadows, but inside Lola and Maurice scrambled and cawed as she unlocked the door. Her hand reached for a familiar light and she dropped her bundle on the table. She turned a light on in each room and greeted Max's paintings like old friends as she moved toward the bedroom. On the far wall, next to the window, his self-portrait glared at her. She glared back, as if they were having words. Was he angry at her for coming back so late in the day or for going to America in the first place? She couldn't tell. There was a glint in his eye that she had not noticed before, a thin splinter of humor that wanted to laugh but took life too seriously to laugh just now. Maybe a moment from now, but not now.

"If you lived your life somewhere else, you might be a happier man," she said out loud. "But you would not be happier in America." He looked back, almost ready to smile, absorbing every word.

Then, slowly, she removed her cotton jacket, her long blue dress, her shiny black slip and stockings, her earrings, her white bra, and panties. The odor of her body filled the room like dusk as she stood defiantly in front of the self-portrait, showing herself with pride. After all, she had now lived longer and gone farther out in the world than he had— all the way to America and back. Then she unpinned her hair and let it hang in matted clumps around her head. She stood there like that for a while, exposed, immodest, letting the self-portrait look her over. "Listen to me," she said. "No one in that place is happier than we were right here. I am your wife and I know what I'm saying." Then she shook her head a little to free the hair that needed combing out, crawled under the sheet with a soft groan as her weight sank into the mattress, and slept for a very long time.

Bicycle Dreams

A boy cannot live without a future. Marcel captured this thought like a butterfly as he walked to the market where he bought and sold fruit to help his mother. He also worked with his father in the banana fields and ran errands for *blancs* who came and went like clouds drifting through long, hot days. Sometimes he got a dollar from a *blanc* and sometimes he saved it, but more often he bought sweets for his brothers and sisters. Once, when he was younger, a *blanc* gave him a pair of shoes out of a back-pack. That time, he sold the gift and gave most of the money to his mother.

The rooms in Marcel's house were crowded but at least we have a house, his father often said. Sometimes his father disappeared for days or weeks but he always came back. We are blessed, his mother said, blessed with strong bones and broad backs, blessed with fat chickens and a garden full of beans. Blessed with a papaya tree in the yard. Life itself is a blessing, she said defiantly. But Marcel was beginning to think bigger thoughts.

Perhaps it was the *blancs* that drove through the village in shiny cars with tinted glass windows or the Haitian police in their fine uniforms that made him want more. Perhaps it was the television screen he saw a few times at the shop in St. Marc, or the glossy posters of bridges and cities at school, left behind by the American cousin of a teacher. At first he thought it was wrong to want more, but then his mind tilted like a bird cutting through air, lifting above the landscape on new wings. Flying there, above the hard work and simple blessings, his mind formed the thought: a boy cannot live without a future. This thought felt so true and so right that he caught his breath and blinked at the sun. For days he kept the thought to himself, held it in his pocket like unspent money. Then, as they were shelling peas behind the house he looked at his little sister, Monique, and said it aloud, "A boy cannot live without a future." She smiled, sucking voraciously on a rod of sugar cane. He shook his head and laughed, how could a stupid little girl begin to understand?

Day and night he kept his new awareness close to his heart. A future was not only important, he reasoned, and not just for special people. It was necessary for *everyone*. From this day on, he told himself, I am living for my future. *And what can you do about it?* A voice from within asked this question three times before Marcel could answer it.

A bicycle, his heart replied. A bicycle makes a difference—a big, important difference. That was obvious. It means a way to get to school. It means a way to make money to pay for school. A bicycle would save time when he went to the market and allow him to carry more fruit in baskets attached with wire to the handlebars, fruit that could be sold, to make money, to pay for school. His heart turned like a wheel spinning *faster faster faster*. That was the beginning, the simple answer to the voice in his head. A bicycle would mean a bigger world. He might even ride it to Port-au-Prince. Imagine that, riding along the highway on a bicycle, arms in the air, his body curving like leaf. He might even find a girl to love and give her a ride on the cross bar, protecting her as they dashed through towns, smelling her hair, telling her secrets in the speed of the wind.

Soon after these thoughts, Marcel began to have bicycle dreams. Each night he would fall asleep with the vision of his bicycle. Each night he would imagine himself pedaling along an empty road, through towns and villages, along the sea. In his dreams he rode his bicycle on an endless road, a road that might even take him all the way to Miami where he would speak English and wear a white shirt and have a house and a job. He had heard people in village talk of Haitians who had gotten that far and become real Americans. He fell asleep to the blue-dark speed of his bicycle dreams and woke up to their soft remembrance telling himself, *I will have a future.*

In daylight, he studied bicycles with a keen-but-concealed interest. His would have thick tires and at least five gears. It would be red or black with chrome trim. He would tend to this beautiful bicycle like his mother tended the garden. Sometimes he would pass a girl on the path on Sunday and smell her soapy skin from four feet away. He smiled, thinking how if he had a bicycle he would give such a girl a ride to church and fill his head with the fruit-sweet odor of her body, holding her shoulders like a blossoming bush in his arms. *And how will you pay for it?* The voice in his head was stern, like his father's. He smiled, silently talking back to that voice. I can earn money, he explained. I can work harder and save money, maybe forty dollars a year if I try, maybe more.

He calculated the cost of limes and plantanes, of papayas and mangoes, of pineapples and melons. How many could he carry from the market? How many could he sell before they spoiled? How much could he charge? How much could he hide in the bottom of his pocket and save? It would take three years, at least, but he was only 15. If he started now he might have a bicycle when he was eighteen. Marcel took a deep breath and stared at the numbers on his paper. Three years was a long time, but time did not matter as much as the bicycle. Red or black. Silver spokes. A stiff basket on the handlebars and a girl with almond eyes cradled in his arms. He had a long time to think about it and a long time to wait, but he was certain that his bicycle would come, and with it the promise of a future.

He worked hard for the next year, giving up school and soccer games. He walked back and forth to the big markets in Pont Sondé and Ti Rivière to get the best prices on mangoes and avocados. Then he walked to the Route Nationale, carrying heavy baskets of fruit and vegetables on his head to sell to missionaries and rich Haitians riding in cars and busses. His shoes cracked and tore at the seams. His neck hurt. Sometimes he worked in the garden too, or in the fields with his father. Sometimes he swept walks and removed seed pods from the sidewalks for doctors and teachers. Little by little he earned money, so that by the time he turned 16 he had thirty four Haitian dollars.

Marcel sat beneath an almond tree on the bench behind his house carefully counting his money. Thirty four dollars. A bicycle would cost six times that. But time did not matter as much as the bicycle or the bicycle dreams that continued, comforting him each night. He had fallen behind in school, but he would make it up one day. He was young. There was plenty of time.

Suddenly he heard a choking sound. He turned to find his mother standing on the step, looking at the garden and weeping. "So dry," she sobbed. "Look!"

He looked and felt a rock drop in his throat. How could he not have noticed this before? Bean plants shriveled and thick with dust. Tomato plants half the normal height. Many things were scarce at the market, but the garden that fed his mother and father and sisters and brothers was barely alive. He stood up and went to her, placing a hand on her arm as she wept.

"Dry season," she hissed. "But worse than last year. Worse every year! We'll need to plant again. But where in the name of God will we find the money to buy new seed?!" She covered her face with her apron, sobbing.

Marcel stood still. Thirty four dollars in his pocket , a sobbing mother, and a dying garden. There was no choice. He took the drawstring bag out of his pocket and gave her all of his money.

At first she looked frightened. "Thirty-four dollars? But how?" Her face tightened. "You didn't steal this did you?! Tell me the truth now! We don't steal nothing from nobody!"

"No, no," he laughed. "I earned it!"

"Earned it?" She was stunned. So she hugged her son, saying God would bless him forever, and tucked the money deep in her pocket. He watched it slide away from her hand, down into that dark hole, quick as a lizard.

Two years later, when Marcel was 18 years old, he sat beneath the same tree counting his money again. Eighty-six Haitian dollars. Half, he reasoned, close enough to start planning. When the time came, he would dress in clean clothes, as if going to church, and spend the morning walking to St. Marc. He would feel proud to pass the market without carrying a basket on his head and another on his back. He would have a restaurant meal then go to the bicycle shop and bargain with the proprietor. If he knew anything, it was how to get a fair price. He would scratch his head, step back, threaten to walk away, stay a bit longer, throw out his hands, and, after a pensive look, he would concede to a little more than half the asking price. By the end of the day, he would own a bicycle and soar homeward like a bird.

At 19, Marcel made a box out of a coconut so he could keep his money safe in his room. The year began slowly, but the dry season was not so bad and there seemed to be more *blancs* in Haiti than ever. He sold them the fattest melons, the tallest pineapples, the best mangoes for high

prices and good tips. He ran errands to buy Coca Cola and
beer for a short lady from a place called Switzerland who gave
him thirty Haitian dollars before she returned to her country,
patting his shoulder and wishing him good luck. Another lady
gave him fifty Haitian dollars for school. He nodded and said
he would spend it on books. By November he realized he had
two hundred Haitian dollars. He took the money out of the
coconut shell box, unfolded it carefully, and arranged it in
stacks in the candlelit darkness of his room. Then he put the
stacks beneath his pillow and slept peacefully, dreaming
bicycle dreams and planning his trip to St. Marc.

The next day he set off at dawn. It was Saturday and
the market at Pont Sondé was just coming alive as he passed.
He waved to an old woman he knew, a spice merchant called
Madame Cinnamon. After the market the road became flat
and rocky. He walked in the field to make it easier, picking up
burrs and clumps of grass in his torn shoes. He thought
about a tap-tap ride to shorten the trip, but decided to save
his money. At last, as the sun rose high in the sky, he saw the
buildings that marked the edge of St. Marc. His feet were
tired but he ran toward the buildings with his arms in the air.
He sat in a restaurant to collect himself, enjoying a plate of
rice with fried pork and beans. He took his time drinking a
Coca-Cola, then ordered another one so he could sit a while
longer. The girl who waited on him smiled shyly as she
cleared his plate, so he left her a good tip for her gentle smile.

As he turned off the square toward the bicycle shop,
he encountered a throng of people pushing toward the
highway. They were moving as one, thick mass, chanting
together, calling for the removal of a man named Dornal.
"Enough is enough!" they called, rolling forward like a wave.
Marcel could not understand who Dornal was or why he
should be removed. He stood for a moment, studying the

crowd then decided to push in the opposite direction through the mass of bodies and voices, making his way to the other side. He pressed forward and squeezed his way through, like a fish swimming upstream. Suddenly, he emerged disheveled, standing alone in the street in front of the bicycle shop.

The bicycle shop proprietor was thickset and bald, a former policeman with a face the color of spilled ink and a fat, pleated forehead. He was known for miles around as Officer Bicyclette. "Bonjour Officer Bicyclette. I am here to buy a bicycle!"

Officer Bicyclette scowled, then showed him three models: a brand new green one with thin tires, a slightly used red one with thick tires, and an old black one with a wide, wobbly seat. They all had silver trim..

"How much?" Marcel asked, pointing to the red one.

"Eighty dollars U.S." Officer Bicyclette was known to think in U.S. dollars ever since he started traveling to Miami to visit his sister. He unlocked the red bicycle and wheeled it to the front of the shop where it gleamed in the afternoon sun.

"How about fifty dollars."

"How about you go to hell."

"Maybe sixty, then."

"Humph!"

"Well, you know, I don't really need this bicycle today." Marcel took a step away. "Say, what's that crowd yelling about anyway?"

"The schoolmaster. They don't like him."

"I donno. Maybe I'd pay sixty-two."

Officer Bicyclette stared at the street, unsmiling. There was a silence between them as Marcel moved around the shop. He touched the handlebars of each bicycle. He smelled the rubber tires. Then, looking up quickly, he made his final offer. "Okay then, if you insist I can pay sixty-four."

"Sixty-five." Officer Bicyclette stared straight ahead as if he were talking to the dust in the road.

Marcel moved toward the beautiful red bicycle, reaching for his pouch of money. Then a rock fell in his throat and his mouth opened. No pouch. No money. Nothing. He slapped his pockets with both hands. Maybe he left it at the restaurant. But no, he remembered the pouch in his hand at the door of the restaurant. Maybe he dropped it in the crowd. Oh no. Was he robbed in that crowd or did squeezing through the crowd force the pouch up and out, onto the street? He ran into the street and looked up and down, studying the footprints left by angry people. There was nothing lying in the road but rocks, dust, and a few shreds of paper. He came back into the shop and took a hold of the bicycle grips. "I seem to have lost my money," he said quietly.

Officer Bicyclette leaned back, staring angrily at Marcel. He was heavy and moved slowly. Suddenly, too suddenly, Marcel lifted the bicycle into the street, mounted it quickly, and pedaled furiously toward the town square and the sea, toward the highway, toward anywhere and everywhere. This is my bicycle, he told himself, pushing hard. I earned it. It is mine, mine, mine! He pedaled into the sun, flying on red and silver wheels. He threw his head back, giving in to a new sensation. This must be joy, he told himself. Or freedom. Whatever it was, this moment was worth everything.

The police were waiting for him at the end of town, standing in the road three across and armed with machine guns. They grabbed him, mid-air, right off the bicycle and threw him on the ground like a sack of flour. They kicked his ribs and hit him with the dull metal butts of their guns. Then they picked him up, chained his wrists, shoved him into a van, and slammed the door shut. He closed his eyes, alone in the darkness.

Marcel remembers the vehicle turning around. It was a turn like a full circle, like the turns he used to make on the soccer field. Then the driver picked up speed and drove a long time on bumpy roads before coming to a screeching halt. Marcel heard music and people talking when they stopped. But the van started up again and drove further, up a hill, down a hill, groaning in darkness, careening left and right until at last it stopped. They pulled him out, from darkness to darkness, and marched him into a hallway with yellow walls and exposed electric light bulbs. At the end of the hallway there was a metal door and behind it a room full of men, most of them young, just like him; most of them half-dressed without shirts or shoes. He stood in the doorway and counted the men the way he used to count his money, stopping at eighty-five. They were sitting on the floor, leaning drowsily against the walls, scratching sores, yawning, or stretched out on the cots that lined the walls and divided the center of the room.

"Where am I?" Marcel asked.

"Welcome to prison!" a voice called out. A group of men playing cards looked up and jeered. "Make yourself at home!"

It is three years later now, three years after that soaring flight through St. Marc and the long, dark ride in the van. Marcel is still there, still in that room with over hundred men. They spend twenty-three hours a day in that room; one hour each day is allotted for air and food. They relieve themselves in metal buckets placed as close as possible to the six windows cut close to the ceiling and covered with iron grates. Some of them have left the room for trials and other prisons. A few have been released. Others have arrived in their place, but it is the same yellow room with the same smell and the same cots pushed against the walls and running down the center.

They sleep in shifts. Marcel has been here long enough now that he gets to sleep at night, from eleven to five a.m. He watches to see when his friend Antoine is stirring, ready to take his turn. Sometimes Marcel sits on the edge of the sagging cot for a while to stake out his rightful place, his chance to rest and dream. He no longer asks when his trial will be held. The last time, he was beaten and denied food for three days. "To hell with that," he told himself.

Antoine blinks and sits up on the cot, looking around like newborn goat. His small eyes are bright with surprise, as if he has never seen this place before. The stench doesn't matter anymore, but the sheer number of backs and legs and glossy heads amazes him. Antoine closes his eyes until Marcel nudges him gently onto his feet. "Come on, now. My turn."

Marcel goes to sleep quickly, disappearing in the sparkling darkness of bicycle dreams. Sometimes the dreams are frightening. Sometimes tires unfurl like serpents and spokes spin out into needles of light. But usually the dreams are joyful as Marcel rides with the sea at his side, a soap-smelling girl balanced in his arms. He is flying in his sleep, soaring in the night, steering toward a smoke-filled village and a mother's garden. His eyes will open soon enough in a room where dreams decompose, where hope is just a particle of memory dancing in a shaft of light. And then another night will come and with it more bicycle dreams because a boy cannot live without a future. Marcel lives for the future every night when he leaves this place in whisper darkness, riding the road of his dreams.

The Wanderer

To the edge of the wood I am drawn, I am drawn,
Where the gray beach glimmering runs, as a belt of the dawn…
Sidney Lanier, "The Marshes of Glynn" (1878)

I

"You *have* to come, Biggy! The weather is looking too good to be true and Henry is only planning to turn 50 once in his life, thank the *Lord*. Fly to Savannah, if you don't want to drive. I'll send someone to pick you up."

Caroline du Bignon had grown accustomed to her nickname and she liked the way Charlene said it with a long whining crescendo of an "eeeee" at the end, just the way Daddy had always done, despite Mother's protests. "Why did we put *Caroline* on the birth certificate anyway if ya'll carry on callin' her 'Biggy'?" Daddy liked it, that's for sure; a tease that stuck primarily because Caroline was not big at all, but naturally small and thin, even if she acted big from the beginning.

"You been a big girl from the big-ginnin'," Daddy said with his hee-haw of a laugh. The contrast between Caroline's stature and personality had struck the whole family early on, including Charlene. "What a BIG mouth!" five year old Charlene would say, when the new baby hollered at anything that moved. Mother could only agree. "That one has a mind of her own. Must be your Daddy's adventurous blood inside those tiny little veins."

It was nearly impossible to dress Caroline up for church without a squabble, which is why Mother gradually gave up on God and took to playing the piano Sunday mornings instead. Chopin. Debussy. She had a fondness for French composers whose melodies wandered over the keys like birds weaving through the air. "Piano music has a calming effect on Caroline," she said. But piano music or not, if summer tourists ventured onto the property it was perfectly normal to hear a child's shriek ringing out from the porch. "This is private property! Can't you READ?"

"Who taught Caroline to be so rude?" Daddy's Aunt Ada asked, a glass of gingerale suspended in midair.

"No idea," Daddy giggled.

Caroline's bad behavior was more or less accepted by the age of three, but when she talked back to the black cleaning lady one day that woman turned around and looked at the child with wild bloodshot eyes. "Who you think you are, Miss Caroline? Some little Biggy, *or whut?*"

Daddy heard the remark and from that moment on, Caroline du Bignon was called "Biggy," at least out there on the island where she became well known among winter residents and local officials as the outspoken younger daughter of Charlie du Bignon, heir and proprietor to a tract of land that had once been a cotton plantation. In Caroline's youth, Charlie was the best lawyer on the island and Mama's flower delivery business got the whole family invited to plenty of parties, weddings, and funerals. "Comb your hair, Caroline. It's nice when a dead person has unexpected guests show up." Mother could be stern-faced as she clutched a bunch of roses wrapped in colored foil. It was her habit to take something extra to funerals. "Respect for the dead, compassion for the temporarily living," she muttered, tugging at Caroline's sleeve.

* * *

"Really, Biggy, you wouldn't want to miss Henry's party, would you?" Charlene's voice had suddenly diminished through the small receiver of the cell phone. She sounded genuinely hurt.

"Oh Char, if it's really so important …"

"Of *course* it's important! What on earth could be *more* important?! My husband is half a century OLD, Biggy! Think about it!"

"Okay, Sis, I'll come down, but only for an overnight. The spring term just ended and there's a pile of work on my desk that has to be done and—"

"Blah blah. You do whatever you want but we want to see you when the champagne pops on Saturday night! I'll have Nellie freshen up the guest house and Clayton will put coffee and breakfast goodies in the kitchen and what else … what else … don't bother with a gift because Henry still hasn't read the last two books you gave him. Damit, I better have the flower bed weeded too because it's a holy mess after the so-called 'April showers'… gale force winds, if you really want to know!"

The guest house. How odd that phrase sounded, even after three years time. It had been a good decision to sell it off to Charlene and Henry, that was certain. The money had allowed Caroline to break free from the island and buy her own condo in Atlanta within walking distance of Emory University where she had taught English literature for over ten years now. "All that sounds fine, Charlene. I'll plan to get in Saturday afternoon and come up to the big house around five o'clock."

"Oh, I meant to tell you, I'll be wearing a tight black cocktail dress, just to see if Henry's got any juice left in him after a half century, my *gawd*!"

"Sounds lovely, Charlene. Just lovely. Thanks for the call. And give my love to Henry."

"Spike heels too, only because we're having the party catered. I couldn't do it all myself and look hot at the same damn time."

"You always look hot, Char. Let me go now. I'll see you next week."

Caroline sat for a moment to recover from the onslaught of her sister's loud, demanding voice. Then she shampooed her hair, as if to rinse her mind of old memories stirred up like an invisible storm swirling deep inside the ocean. Caroline had come to detest these trips to the island even before Daddy died and Mother's mind started to wander. With Anne du Bignon's death two-and-a-half years ago, there was no longer any point in pretending the island was some kind of paradise, even if the gray beaches and wind-twisted trees were still beautiful in their own eternal way. Most of it had been condemned, commercialized, carved up, and sold off to the highest bidder for the second time in little over a hundred years.

Caroline walked on the beach after the funeral service "to breathe the salt air and shake off a headache," she said. But really, it was to say farewell to all the days she had spent there, to look out at the green mark on the horizon that was Cumberland Island and imagine the open sea beyond. It was November then and she was glad to be alone on the beach with her own quiet thoughts of Mother and the endless flower arrangements she had made and delivered. How odd the way it all mingled into one vast garden of memory; thorns and clipped branches, driftwood "accents."

It was only during her college years that Jeyll Island started to feel like a family of ghosts softly beckoning, beginning with the drive down Horton Road where a plaque honoring "Christophe-Anne Poulain du Bignon (1739-1825)" seemed to mark a boundary that Caroline did not want to cross. How long would she live within the confines of family history, she wondered? How permanent was the stamp of greed that had made the du Bignons owners of this island and over 400 slaves by 1800? She imagined Mother and Daddy's property deserted, as Union troops had found it during the Civil War. She remembered the way a shadow had fallen across her parents' eyes whenever she asked questions. Certain topics were "not discussable," Mother said. The faint foundations of the old slave cottages were "not discussable." Nor was the fake cemetery where ancestral bones were glorified but not actually buried, and no one seemed to know where those people were buried. Walls built with African hands and houses restored with what Daddy referred to as "our hard-earned fortune" had been reinvented as local monuments, noble evidence of historic preservation. But the real lives that had lived there and been so willfully forgotten were too real for Caroline.

"No! No! It's not *real* anymore," Charlene insisted. "It's NOT!" As a legend equivalent to the *Mutiny on the Bounty*, Charlene du Bignon Tutlow had remained impressed by Captain du Bignon's brilliant naval career and his narrow escape from the poverty of Brittany in the wake of the French Revolution. She admired his legendary courage and resourcefulness in the purchase of two barrier islands in the southern United States. Eventually, he owned the whole of Jekyll Island, a fact that Charlene stated with an air of self-righteousness. Charlene du Bignon Tutlow loved her ancestors as much as Caroline had learned to detest them, both for the same reasons.

"It's in the past, Caroline," Henry would say, letting his heavy jaw sag a bit as it did when he had to much to drink. "Who gives a damn anymore, anyway?"

Time had passed and among the islands off the coast of Georgia "Jekyll" had developed into a winter retreat for robber barons at the turn of the last century, and then a comfortable middle-class vacation spot nicely situated between Jacksonville and Savannah. No one spoke any longer about the Captain's business interests in oak forests or of the slaves he purchased from West Africa to make a go of the cotton plantation. And certainly no one spoke of the du Bignon descendants who dared to purchase one of the last "inventories" of slaves, a cargo of nearly 500 men and women who arrived on Jekyll Island in 1858, sweltering and starving down in the hold of a ship called *The Wanderer*. "That's the worst thing," Caroline would say, "to know that our relatives brought the last slave ship onto American soil."

Charlene groaned whenever they fell into this conversation, which they had done about 20 times in the past 20 years. "That's just a bunch of old sad history, Biggy! Anyway, *we* didn't do it, did we? Why do you want *me* to feel bad, li'l sister?"

"No, we didn't do it, that's right, but it's something more than history, Char. History is not just history anyway. It's real people, people like us, and it's still part of us, like it or not, believe it or not."

"It's in the golly-damned *past*, Caroline." Each word was announced with fervent authority. "Furthermore, we have three lovely old houses down here and the gardeners are working like mad to keep it no less than gorgeous and we want you to come and be golly-damn happy *with us* and *for us* once in a while, if that's not too much to ask."

Caroline smiled weakly at her sister's sense of entitlement. "I like it better when you call me Biggy."

* * *

The drive from northeast Atlanta to the Georgia coast was long; over five hours, with two stops, through the bland yellow heat of south Georgia. Caroline turned up the AC and listened to half an audio book of Judi Dench reading Yeats by the time she got to Macon, then there was time for two rhythm and blues CDs before stopping for gas in the nowheresville of Hazelhurst. After that, the earth on either side of the road gave way to sandy soil as she approached Glynn County. The foliage changed too as pines began to mingle with palms and low-slung houses straggled along the route, each with a small patio or a screened in porch.

The Downing Musgrove Causeway connecting the town of Brunswick to the island had always been processional for Caroline, like marching straight-backed down the aisle at Commencement. These six miles of paved road cut through 4,000 acres of salt marsh and mudflats. She had always known that watery world on either side of the road concealed shorebirds and insects living deep in golden grass and damp earth. The Marshes of Glynn separated the world back there from the island up ahead, the island that contained the emotional cargo of Caroline's life like the hull of a ship. There were stopping points along the causeway; restaurants, souvenir shops, and viewing points for bird watchers. There were always walkers out there at the three mile mark who seemed to be going nowhere; tanned people with jackets and hair flapping wildly like exotic birds who had lost their inner compass. Caroline's favorite spot was the place where she remembered coming to watch snow white egrets with Mother at twilight. "Those birds glow like candles in the evening light," Mother said as they drove back onto the island through a darkening tunnel of live oaks. "They really do just glow, don't they?"

* * *

Caroline clicked the automatic garage door opener and waved to a black man pushing a wheelbarrow of weeds away from the guest house. She put her canvas tote bag on the kitchen counter and stood for a moment in the sand-colored living room, feeling cool air circulating silently around her. The covered patio on the other side of a sliding glass door was swept clean and, beyond it, an arc of green lawn seemed to rise up like a stage flecked with light in front of a curtain of tall trees. On the other side of that curtain was a golf course, barely visible from the guest house; Daddy had always referred to that expanse of green as "crew cut grass." Like Mother, he preferred the wilder side of the island with its windswept trees, gnarled driftwood, and tangled debris washed up by the waves.

Caroline had walked those seemingly empty beaches with both of her parents, searching out tiny fossilized shells imprinted in stone. "Lookie here!" Daddy would call out. "Look right there, that's a genuine fossil!" That was exciting. But here, gazing into a wall of trees, Caroline felt no sensation at all; no excitement or joy; no nostalgia or curiosity for what might be concealed by the tall vertical trunks wearing sleeves of dark green. The problem is *knowing*, she thought to herself, *knowing* what was there before the golf club and the timeshare development, before the indoor tennis court was built, before millionaires made this place elegant and enviable then lost it all.

Caroline pulled her gaze back and smiled at the porous white rock in the center of the patio table. When Charlene redecorated the house she agreed to include a few mementoes of Caroline's travels to Australia, Ireland, and the Caribbean. Other islands, each with another story to tell. She touched the rock and remembered finding it on the island of Aruba full of fine, white sand. She remembered handing it to Charlene who studied it for a moment before placing it in the center of the table. "It's not from around here, but I suppose no one will mind," she said, pressing her lips shut as if another word might start a war. An image of Charlene's slightly irritated face floated in proximity to the rock, as if the glass table reflected old memories. Was it the presence of an aggressive little sister, a "Biggy," that had planted resistance in those eyes and caused them to harden over the years? In childhood, Charlene had been the one with manners and social graces. "We are du Bignons!" she had announced early on. "We are *supposed* to be polite to *everybody*, even people we don't like."

That lecture was first delivered after Caroline stuck her tongue out at a teen-age boy who claimed a square meter of sand with his towel, shaking the sandy rag in Caroline's eyes to shoo her away. "Polite to *everybody*?" Caroline asked, dumbstruck. "Even *stupid* people like *that*?"

"Even stupid people like that, li'l sister. That's how it is." Charlene yanked Caroline's arm, dragging her down the beach. "Just let him be and we'll move along."

It wasn't long after that when Mother sat them both down on the porch of the big house with a pitcher of iced tea and said, "There's something I need to tell you girls about your ancestors." It was clear, even then, that Mother and

Charlene had already had a talk about those long-dead people and their illegal ship, that heavy vessel called *The Wanderer* that unloaded slaves on Jekyll Island 50 years after the importation of slaves was declared illegal. "Especially *you*, Caroline. *You* need to know a little bit of history so you can behave appropriately."

"I *am* appropriate."

"Shut-up and listen to Mother."

Looking back, it was probably at that moment that Caroline decided she'd rather not be a part of this family after all. She had seen plenty of books in the bookshop in Brunswick and thought she ought to write a book some day, maybe a history book about whatever there was out there, lying deep beneath the marsh or the sea. Or maybe something about a French castle or an English garden. Somehow, she knew that if she stayed too long on Mother and Daddy's porch with her every move scrutinized and reported on by Charlene, her book would never see the light of day.

"I *already* behave appropriately," she said. "But you go ahead, Mother, and tell me about my ancestors."

Mother frowned and Charlene rolled her eyes toward Heaven as she wheeled into her little sister like a pickup truck sliding into a ditch. "Listen up, Biggy! We've all had enough of your back talk! No more, you hear? NO MORE!" Charlene was fed up. That was clear enough and things had hardly changed since.

II

The child emerged out of the trees like the shadow of a misplaced water bird, a heron or an egret, perhaps, except that egrets are white and this angular shape was as black as a wet branch. He was small too, and thin, little more than a vertical movement that shimmered through fused light and shaggy trees. Caroline's eyes settled on the solid part of the shadow pushing through those dappled threads of light, watching closely as mere form became condensed into something else. It was a child. Plain as day. A dark child, with boney arms and legs. A child, wearing a faded green checkered shirt and pants the color of wet sand. Only later would she notice his pink plastic sandals, one torn so that the right heel flapped outward. What she did see from the patio, and what made this form human, were the eyes that seemed to weigh heavy inside his head, a large head resembling a skull topped off with a nimbus of rust-colored bristles. Caroline stifled a scream and stepped back. But why should she be frightened by a child, by a little boy who had probably lost his way in the pine forest? He stood still and she stared at him, a skinny little boy on the edge of a too-green lawn too cut too neatly in accordance with Charlene's instructions.

"Hello?" She called the word as a question but the child did not reply. "I said *hello*. Are you deaf?"

"*Allo*," he said, but only half as loud as Caroline's sharp voice.

"Allo. What's that? Is that French?"

The child stood still, staring, as Caroline shifted gears and summoned up her passable French. "*J'ai dit allo à toi. Tu parles français?*" She waited a moment to see if he understood her words: I said hello to you. Do you speak French?

"*Un peu*," he replied.

"A little?"

"*Petit petit.*"

Caroline nodded and the child stepped forward into lemon-colored light, then stopped as if ordered not to cross an invisible line. He seemed harmless but Caroline kept her eyes fixed on him all the same. What if he was some kind of a decoy, a distraction planted in backyards while grown-up thieves lurked in the forest or surrounded the house? She turned suddenly for a flash glance at the front door. She could see the deadbolt in place and the garage door had locked automatically. "Where do you come from? *D'où viens-tu?*"

The child pushed his lower lip forward, as if he had to think carefully about his reply. He was a cautious child, a child who knew something of his origins and how they might be perceived. "*Mwen vwajé,*" he said.

"*Un voyagé?* A wanderer?"

"*Wi.*" He spoke in a soft voice that was almost a whisper.

"*Oui?* You say yes? A wanderer from where? From faraway? *De loin?*"

"*Ayiti, Madame.*"

Ayiti. Ayiti. Caroline walked to the edge of the flagstone patio and peered into the eyes of that child, taking care not to leave the surface of stone. "Do you mean *Haiti?*" He took another step forward but remained on the grass. That was when she noticed the loose sandal. 'Haiti,' she mumbled. 'Could he truly have come all the way up here from Haiti?' The language he spoke was not French, after all, but something like it, something close. Some kind of Créole. She waited, remembering an article about a boatload of Haitians that had made it to the coast of Florida, south of Jacksonville, just last week. Could this child have been on that boat? But how would he get here? Hitching a ride, maybe? Hiding in another boat? Clinging to the underbelly of a delivery truck?

"Haiti," she said clearly, as if announcing the winner of an Academy Award. Poorest Country on Earth: and the winner is, Haiti!

He held his body straight, the cage of his chest pushed out like a toy soldier. He smiled a broad smile of recognition that revealed square teeth too large for his mouth. Then he took a deep breath and spoke clearly with a surprising gust of national pride. *"Wi, Madame. Ayiti."*

* * *

Now really, she told herself, there certainly is no harm in feeding a hungry child. He was obviously hungry, judging from the way he worked fast to fill his mouth with milk and cereal, as if the food might be snatched away any minute. Then she brought out a bunch of bananas someone had put in the kitchen. *"Pour toi,"* she said. "For you." He smiled and ate three without stopping. Caroline felt an odd pleasure watching the boy now seated on the upholstered patio settee eating so joyfully. His needs were simple and she marveled at her power to fulfill them.

"I am Caroline," she said. *"Je m'appelle Caroline. Et toi?"*

"Charlemagne!" he said. Once again his chest ballooned as he smiled with a mouthful of banana mash.

"Charlemagne, the great king. *Le grand roi, Charlemagne?"*

The boy swallowed the last puddle of milk from his cereal bowl and laughed out loud, shaking his head. *"Non, Madame! Mwen vwajé!* No way, lady! I am a wanderer!"

They sat together for a while, not speaking at all. Then Caroline went inside and brought out a beach towel. He looked tired, but maybe it wasn't a good idea to leave him out on the patio alone. What if Clayton or the gardener came around to check on her? They would chase the boy away; might even slap him or kick him to scare him off. He smiled at her with heavy lids, dozing a little with his hand on his belly. She watched him as she had watched birds with Mother, taking in his movements, his form, his instinctive breathing as he leaned toward the edge of sleep. She tapped her foot nervously, making a sharp sound that seemed to startle him. "*Viens avec moi,*" she said. "Come with me." He blinked and looked around. Then, catching on as she extended her hand, he followed her into the kitchen where she offered him a paper towel. He wiped his face with it and smiled. Then she led him out to the garage where her car was still warm from the long drive. She opened the back seat and tossed in the beach towel. "*Reste ici. Je reviens.*" she said. "You stay here until I come back."

He looked inside the car and smiled. "*Kay mwen?*" He was confused, his eyes wide as she made a fan-like gesture of invitation with her left-hand. "My house?" he asked.

"For you. *Pour toi.*" She swept the air with her hand until he understood.

"*Mesi, Madame.*" The child's thanks were whispered as he climbed into the back of Caroline's du Bignon's silver Toyota and rested his head on the towel.

"*Reste ici,* ok?"

The child nodded with soft eyes and went to sleep.

III

Sounds of piano jazz, clinking glasses, and cocktail chatter bubbled off the terrace of Charlene and Henry Tutlow's three-story "cottage," spilling over the white tent erected on the lawn for the occasion. Caroline had walked ten minutes along a private path edged in pine bark and azalea bushes to get from the pink-shuttered guest house to the main house. As she made her way up the sloping lawn, she wondered what she would do with the child later this evening. She resolved not to stay too long at the party, to spend an hour or so, primarily near Charlene, then claim a splitting headache. The little boy would awaken and realize that he was locked in the garage. What if he had to pee? What if he screamed? Caroline freshened her lipstick before entering the big house in her blue flowered sundress and silver slingbacks. She was greeted at the door by a once-familiar black man in a white dinner jacket—"Good evenin' Miss Caroline!"—just before Charlene came rushing toward her with crystal glasses of champagne, one in each hand.

"Biggy! You made it! Bless your sweet 'ole heart! Here, have a little champagne just to get started."

Caroline kissed her sister's cheek and took one of the glasses. "You look great, Char. Congratulations and happy birthday and all that."

"Biggy!" It was Henry, looking jaunty and nautical in a navy blue jacket and striped silk tie, charmingly gray at the temples and smelling of sandlewood. "Thanks for coming, Big. And I know you know and we all know you didn't have a choice!" They laughed a little and embraced quickly, allowing a few drops of champagne to splash on the carpet.

"I wouldn't miss it, Hank. Happy birthday. But you're damn right, my big sister wouldn't take no for an answer!"

They sighed together in familial unison then moved into the crowd with Charlene pausing to introduce Caroline to every other person between the front door and what Mother used to call the "salon." The baby grand piano was still there, polished like a black mirror, with a jovial man in a tuxedo at the keys. "He takes requests, honey, and he knows every tune that's been written in the past fifty years!"

"Make it one hundred years," the pianist quipped, hands still playing—"You must remember this, a kiss is still a kiss..."—Charlene hummed along for a moment then stopped suddenly. "Look! It's the Havertys come all the way down from Myrtle Beach! Henry, the Havertys!" And in a moment, both Charlene and Henry were hurrying toward the front door, leaving Caroline alone in the crowd.

She wandered through the voices, half smiling at half familiar faces, relinquishing her crystal glass to a girl in a white apron, then selecting artful *canapés* from silver trays carried by expressionless black servants. She moved out to the terrace and looked out across the expanse of manicured lawn bordered in gardenia and hibiscus. She went down dark green steps toward the tent with its Arthurian turrets and plastic Palladian windows, following garlands of English Ivy and sweetheart roses strung over a green outdoor carpet. Piano music receded as Charlene's hoot and call shot out of the house now and then, like a bird trapped inside.

What if he wakes up frightened? What if he needs a bath? Caroline's mind worked over the image of the boy's large eyes and skinny arms. He was dirty and hot and tired. Of course he would need a bath, or at least a chance to run the hose over his body. But what would he wear if his clothes got wet? She winced at the thought of his dark shriveled body without clothes. She had never seen a little black boy without clothes and did not want to put herself in the position of removing his shorts.

"Miss du Bignon! How lovely to see you." It was Eunice Clampton the woman who had looked after Mother in the last year of her life. "I think of you often. How *are* you?" Caroline struggled to talk about herself, her life in Atlanta, her students, her plan to travel to England this summer and do some research on the pre-Raphaelites. She had to shout to be heard in the growing crush of voices and laughter, and her head was throbbing with images of the little Haitian boy sleeping in the back seat of her car. Eunice smiled, hearing very little and understanding even less, finally interrupting the disjointed monologue with exaggerated enthusiasm. "That sounds wonderful! And I wish you the very best! I really, really do!"

Caroline ate three deviled eggs, a chicken wing dipped in hot mustard sauce, tasted a piece of fried okra, and held a position near the *crudités* for a long time, nibbling on grape tomatoes and carrot sticks. A large woman the color of milk chocolate pushed her way through in search of used toothpicks, dirty glasses, and stained napkins. Another brought fresh trays of food and removed the ones that had been picked over. "Don't nobody like celery," she said, lifting a tray high above a hundred heads and slipping out the side flaps of the tent. Caroline followed. There was a man there with a rolling trash can full of dirty plastic plates and chicken bones. The woman with the tray of celery was laughing with him when Caroline suddenly appeared.

"Hep you?" the woman asked. Caroline froze at the question, mouth half open. Help? Yes, help. Please help, she wanted to say. Help me save that child. Help me do something good and courageous. Help me undo what others have done. But she said nothing.

"You all right, m'am?" The man with the trash can jutted his head forward and peered into her eyes.

* * *

The child was still asleep when she got back to the guesthouse, a small dark mass crumpled into a blue towel embroidered with bright yellow moons and metallic stars. The door to the back seat was still open and she shut it carefully, almost silently. Then she went back into the house and changed out of her party dress, folding it neatly to fit in the tote bag. She took two cans of Coca-Cola out of the refrigerator and put them in the tote, along with a box of crackers and two more bananas. She glanced at the clock: 9 p.m. If they left soon, they would be home by 2 a.m. Two thirty, at the latest. The traffic would be light and the neighbors sound asleep. He was small enough to carry and he would understand the meaning of "Ssshhhh!" She looked at him as she lifted the tote bag onto the floor. He was motionless, except for the rise and fall of his belly glistening in the light.

Tomorrow would come, of course, with dawn encircling them like a ribbon. At that point she would have to think more clearly and make some decisions. She did not want to call the police or an embassy or an immigration office, that much was certain. She might call a lawyer or a colleague or a friend. The truth of it was that she did not want to let that child go. One person ought to be able to save one child, she thought. What good is all of *this* if I can't do *that*? She wondered what all of *this* might be. A college education? Inherited wealth? What kind of success had she made of her life anyway? She wiped her eyes and took an aspirin because, after all, she really did feel some kind of a pressure in her head, some kind of relentless rhythm like a drum beating in the night. It will end, she told herself. The pain will end and a solution will be found. I will buy him some clothes and make him strong and fix his teeth. They might wander together in unknown territory for awhile, but not forever. Because sooner or later, this would feel normal—this moment when she decided to save one child.

Caroline looked through the car window and smiled. He was still asleep, his chest quivering a little like a small animal, his arms fallen back in a tender, defenseless gesture of trust. She got into the driver's seat and opened the garage door automatically, turned the key in the ignition, and rolled backward onto the blacktop that looked like satin in the moonlight. They would drive half the night, but what did that matter? When he woke up she would give him a soda and stop somewhere so he could pee. He is a *vwajé*, she told herself, and so am I. We are wanderers so we know how to keep going.

She aimed the car south then turned right onto the causeway that cut across the Marshes of Glynn with its hidden nests and dark pools, away from the sea and the gray beach, into the darkness. She drove with the window open and her hair flying softly in the humid air of the night. She was half way to Macon before she noticed the stars and the scythe of a white moon in the sky. Daddy used to point to the moon and the stars from the lawn on summer nights, telling old stories of celestial navigation that had come down from the one who arrived here first, over 200 years ago. "The night sky is the best map there is, Biggy—best way to tell where the hell you're goin'." Caroline looked up, remembering that voice, and for the first time in a long time, she knew.